The Zankiwank & The Bletherwitch

S. J. Adair Fitz-Gerald

Arthur Rackham

Alpha Editions

This edition published in 2021

ISBN : 9789354411953

Design and Setting By
Alpha Editions
www.alphaedis.com
Email - info@alphaedis.com

As per information held with us this book is in Public Domain.
This book is a reproduction of an important historical work. Alpha Editions
uses the best technology to reproduce historical work in the same manner
it was first published to preserve its original nature. Any marks or number
seen are left intentionally to preserve its true form.

THE ZANKIWANK & THE BLETHERWITCH

BY S.J. ADAIR FITZGERALD

WITH PICTURES BY ARTHUR RACKHAM

LONDON J.M. DENT & CO
ALPINE HOUSE E.C. 1896

To
MY BLANCHE
I AFFECTIONATELY INSCRIBE
THIS LITTLE BOOK

CONTENTS

PART I
A Trip to Fable Land 1

PART II
The Fairies' Feather and Flower Land . 33

PART III
A Visit to Shadow Land 91

PART IV
The Land of Topsy Turvey 119

LIST OF ILLUSTRATIONS

	PAGE
EVERYBODY MADE A RUSH FOR THE TRAIN *Frontispiece*	
THE ZANKIWANK AND THE BLETHERWITCH . *Title Page*	
THE JACKARANDAJAM	5
MR SWINGLEBINKS	7
THEY WERE RUN INTO BY A DEMON ON A BICYCLE .	17
BIRDS, BEASTS AND FISHES WERE HURRYING BY IN CONFUSING MASSES	19
THE FROGS . . . PLAYING "KISS IN THE RING" .	24
THEY WERE GLUED TO THE EARTH . . .	27
THE ELFIN ORCHESTRA	37
I HAVE DISPATCHED THE JACKARANDAJAM AND MR SWINGLEBINKS IN A FOUR-WHEELED CAB	41
A COMPANY OF FAIRIES . . . LEAPT FROM THE PETALS OF THE FLOWERS	45
THE SLY JACKDAWS AND THE RAVENS . . . EVIDENTLY PLOTTING MISCHIEF	51
ONE OF THE PRETTIEST DANCES YOU EVER SAW .	55
TITANIA ARRIVED . . . WITH A FULL TRAIN OF FAIRIES AND ELVES	61
WILLIE PINCHED HIS EXCEEDINGLY THIN LEGS, MAKING HIM JUMP AS HIGH AS AN APRIL RAINBOW	64
PEASEBLOSSOM AND MUSTARD SEED . . .	71
QUEEN TITANIA AND HER COURT OF FAIRIES WERE EATING PUDDINGS AND PIES	75
THE TWO CHILDREN TUMBLED OFF NOTHING INTO A VACANT SPACE	79

List of Illustrations

	PAGE
"KEEP THE POT A-BOILING," BAWLED THE ZANKIWANK	83
SO INTO SHADOWLAND THEY TUMBLED	87
A WHOLE SCHOOL OF CHILDREN FOLLOWING MADLY IN THEIR WAKE	95
THE GOBLINS STARTED OFF ON HORSEBACK	101
"THE UNFORTUNATE DOLL"	103
THE WINNY WEG WAS DANCING IN A CORNER ALL BY HERSELF	106
MAUDE AND WILLIE WERE RECLINING PEACEFULLY ON A GOLDEN COUCH WITH SILVER CUSHIONS	107
A GAME OF LEAP-FROG	108
A GREAT RED CAVERN OPENED AND SWALLOWED UP EVERYTHING	117
"NOW THEN, MOVE ON!"	123
THE WIMBLE AND THE WAMBLE	126
JORUMGANDER THE YOUNGER . . . APPROACHED THEM WITH A CASE OF PENS	133
"WHY, HERE HE IS!"	138
THE ZANKIWANK ARGUING WITH THE CLERK OF THE WEATHER AND THE WEATHER COCK	145
TIME WAS MEANT FOR SLAVES	151
CHILDREN WITH THE ODDEST HEADS AND FACES EVER SEEN	158, 159
IT WAS A SORT OF SKELETON	163
THE GRIFFIN AND THE PHŒNIX	170
THEY SPRANG INTO THE HASH	173
DR PAMPLETON	177
NO ONE INDIVIDUAL GOT HIS OWN PROPER LIMBS FASTENED TO HIM	183
THERE WAS JOHN OPENING THE CARRIAGE DOOR FOR THEM TO GET OUT	187

Part I

A Trip to Fable Land

By the Queen-Moon's mystic light,
By the hush of holy night,
By the woodland deep and green,
By the starlight's silver sheen,
By the zephyr's whispered spell,
Brooding Powers Invisible,
Faerie Court and Elfin Throng,
Unto whom the groves belong,
And by Laws of ancient date,
Found in Scrolls of Faerie Fate,
Stream and fount are dedicate.
Whereso'er your feet to-day
Far from haunts of men may stray,
We adjure you stay no more
Exiles on an alien shore,
But with spells of magic birth
Once again make glad the earth.

PHILIP DAYRE.

A Trip to Fable Land

"WELL," said the Zankiwank as he swallowed another jam tart, "I think we had better start on our travels at once."

They were all standing under the clock at Charing Cross Station when the station was closed and everybody else had departed, except the train which the Zankiwank had himself chartered. It was all so odd and strange, and the gathering was so very motley, that if it had been to-morrow morning instead of last night, Willie and Maude would certainly have said they had both been dreaming. But, of course, they were not dreaming because they were wide-awake and dressed. Besides, they remembered Charing Cross Station quite well, having started therefrom with their father and mother only last summer when they went to the sea-side for their holidays—and what jolly times they had on the sands! So Maude said promptly, "It is not Night-mare or Dreams or Anything. We don't know what it is, but we must not go to sleep, Willie, in case anything should happen."

Willie replied that he did not want to go to sleep any more. "I believe it's a show," he added, "and somebody's run away with us. How lovely! I'm glad we are lost. Let us go and ask that tall gentleman, who looks like the parlour-tongs in a bathing-suit, to give us some more buns." For, being a boy, he could always eat buns, or an abundance of them, only I hope you won't tell the nursery governess I told you.

It was the Zankiwank, who was doing some conjuring tricks for the benefit of the Jackarandajam and Mr Swinglebinks, to whom Willie referred. The Zankiwank was certainly a very curious person to look at. He had very long legs, very long arms, and a very small body, a long neck and a head like a peacock. He was not wearing a bathing suit as Willie imagined, because there were tails to his jacket, hanging down almost to his heels. He wore a sash round his waist, and his clothes were all speckled as though he had been peppered with the colours out of a very large kaleidoscope. The Jackarandajam was also rather tall and thin, but dressed in the very height of fashion, with a flower in his coat and a cigarette in his mouth, which he never smoked because he never lit it. He was believed by all the others—you shall know who all the others were presently—to know more things than the Man-in-the-Moon, because he nearly always said something that nobody else ever

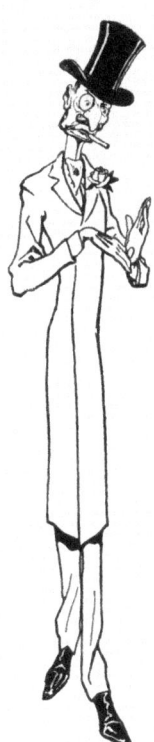

thought of. And the Man-in-the-Moon knows more things than the Old Woman of Mars. You have naturally heard all about Mars—at least, if you have not heard all about her, you all have heard about her, which is just the same thing, only reversed.

> There was an Old Woman of Mars
> Who'd constantly say "Bless my stars,
>   There's the Sun and the Moon
>   And the Earth in a swoon,
> All dying for par-tic-u-lars-u-lars!
> Of this planet of mine called Mars!"

Mr Swinglebinks, unlike his two companions, was short, stout, and dreadfully important. In Fable Land, where we are going as soon as we start for that happy place, he kept a grocer's shop once upon a time. As nobody cared a fig for his sugar and currants, however, he retired from business and took to dates and the making of new almanacks, and was now travelling about for the benefit of his figures. He was very strong on arithmetic, and could read, write, and arithmetise before he went to school, so he never went at all.

While the Zankiwank was talking to his friends an unseen porter rang an unseen bell, and called out in an unknown tongue:—

"Take your seats for Fableland,
Which stands upon a Tableland,
And don't distress the guard.

And when you pass the Cableland
Say nothing to the Gableland
Because it hurts the guard."

"We must put that porter back in the bottle," said the Jackarandajam, "we shall want some bottled porter to drink on the road."

"Well," said Maude, "what a ridiculous thing to say. We don't bottle railway porters, I am sure."

"I wish the Bletherwitch would come," exclaimed the Zankiwank, "we shall miss the next train. She is most provoking. She promised to be here three weeks ago, and we have been waiting ever since."

This astounding statement quite disturbed Willie, who almost swallowed a bun in his excitement. Had he and Maude been waiting there three weeks as well? What would they think at home? You see Maude and Willie, who were brother and sister, had been on a visit to their grandmama; and on their way home they had fallen asleep in the carriage, after having repeated to each other all the wonderful fairy tales their grandmama had related to them. How long they had slept they could not guess, but when they woke up, instead of finding themselves at home in St George's Square, they discovered that they were at Charing Cross Station. Mary, their nurse, had disappeared, so had John the coachman, and it was the Zankiwank who had opened the door and assisted them to alight, saying at the same time most politely—

"I assist you to alight, because it is so dark."

Then he gave them buns and chocolates, ice-creams, apples, pears, shrimps and cranberry tarts. So it stands to reason that after such a mixture they were rather perplexed. However, they did not seem very much distressed, and as they were both fond of adventures, especially in books, they were quite content to accept the Zankiwank's offer to take them for a ride in the midnight-express to Fable Land, over which, as everybody knows, King Æsop reigns. Maudie was nine and a half and Willie was eight and a quarter. Very nice ages indeed, unless you happen to be younger or older, and then your own age is nicer still.

"I think," said the Zankiwank, "that we will start without the Bletherwitch. She knows the way and can take a balloon."

"If she takes a balloon she will lose it. You had better let the balloon take her," exclaimed the Jackarandajam severely.

"Take your places! Take your places!" cried the unseen porter. So everybody made a rush for the train, and they all entered a Pullman Car and sat down on the seats.

"Dear me! How very incorrectly that porter speaks. He means, of course, that the seats should take, or receive us."

The Zankiwank only smiled, while Mr Swinglebinks commenced counting up to a hundred, but as he lost one, he could only count up to ninety-nine—so, to keep his arithmetic going, he subtracted a time-piece from his neighbour's pocket, multiplied his foot-warmers, and divided his attention between the Wimble and the Wamble, who were both of the party, being left-handed and deaf.

Maudie and Willie took their places in the car with all the other passengers amid a perfect babel of chattering and laughing and crying, and then, as the train began to slowly move out of the station, the Zankiwank solemnly sang the following serious song :—

OFF TO FABLE LAND.

The midnight train departs at three,
    To Fable Land we go,
For this express is nothing less
    Than a steamer, don't you know!
We're sailing now upon the Thames,
    All in a penny boat,
And we soon shall change for a mountain range,
    In the atmosphere to float!

    So off we go to Fable Land—
        (Speak kindly to the guard!)
    Which many think a Babel-land,
        But this you disregard.
    You'll find it is a Stable-land,
        With stables in the yard—

A possible, probable, Able-land,
    So do not vex the guard!

We've left behind us Charing Cross,
    And all the town in bed;
For it is plain, though in this train,
    We're standing on our head!
We're riding now in Bedfordshire,
    Which is the Land of Nod;
And yet in the sky we are flying high,
    Which seems extremely odd!

So off we go to Fable Land—
    (Speak kindly to the guard!)
Which many think a Babel-land,
    But this you disregard.
You'll find it is a Stable-land,
    With stables in the yard—
A possible, probable, Able-land,
    So do not vex the guard!

Maudie and Willie found themselves joining lustily in the chorus when the Zankiwank pulled the cord communicating with the guard, and, opening the window, climbed out on to the top of the carriage calling all the time:—

"Guard! Guard! Guard!
Don't go so hard,
　Just give the brake a hitch!
To Charing Cross return—
Nay, do not look so stern—
For I would not tell a cram,
I must send a telegram,
　To my darling little Bletherwitch."

So the guard turned the train round, and they went back to Charing Cross as quick as lightning.

"It's my fault," moaned the Jackarandajam, "I ought to have reminded you. Never mind, we will put on another engine."

So the Zankiwank got out and sent a telegram to the Bletherwitch, and desired her to follow on in a balloon.

Again they started, and everybody settled down until the train reached the British Channel, when it dived through a tunnel into an uninhabited country, where the post-office clerk popped his head into the carriage window and handed in a telegram.

"*From the Bletherwitch,*
　　　To the Zankiwank.
Don't wait tea. Gone to the Dentists."

"Extremely thoughtful," exclaimed everybody. But the Zankiwank wept, and explained to the sympathetic Maude that he was engaged to be married to the Bletherwitch, and he had been waiting for her for fourteen years. "Such a charming creature. I will introduce you when she comes. Fancy, she is only two feet one inch and one third high. Such a suitable height for a bride."

"What," expostulated Willie and Maude together, "she's no bigger than our baby! And you are quite——"

"Eight feet and one half of an inch."

"How disproportionate! It seems to me to be a most unequal match," answered Maude. "What does her mother say?"

"Oh, she hasn't got any mother, you know. That would not do. She has been asleep for two thousand years, and has only just woke up to the fact that I am her destiny."

"She is only joking," declared Maude. "Two thousand years! She *must* be joking!"

"No," replied the Zankiwank somewhat sadly, "she is not joking. She never jokes. She is of Scottish descent," he added reflectively. "I hope she will keep her appointment. I am afraid she is rather giddy!——"

"Giddy! Well, if she has waited two thousand years before making up her mind to go to the dentists she must be giddy. I am afraid you are not speaking the truth."

Before any reply could be given the Guard came to the window and said they would have to go back to Charing Cross again as he forgot to pay his rent, and he always paid his rent on Monday.

"But this is *not* Monday," said Willie. "Yesterday was Monday. To-day is to-morrow you know, therefore it is Tuesday. Pay your landlady double next Monday and that will do just as well."

The Guard hesitated.

"Don't vex the Guard," they all said in chorus.

"I am not vexed," said the Guard, touching his hat. "Do you think it would be right to pay double? You see my landlady is single. She might not like it."

"Write 'I. O. U.' on a post-card and send it to her. It will do just as well, if not better," suggested Mr Swinglebinks.

So the Guard sent the post-card; but in his agitation he told the engineer driver to go straight ahead instead of round the corner. The consequence was that they were run into by a Demon on a bicycle, and thrown out of the train down a coal mine. Luckily there were no coals in the mine so it did not matter, and they went boldly forward—that is to say, Willie and Maude did, and knocked at the front door of a handsome house that suddenly appeared before them.

Nobody opened the door, so they walked in. They looked behind them, but could not see the Zankiwank or any of the passengers in the train; therefore, not knowing what else to do, they went upstairs. They appeared to be walk-

ing up stairs for hours without coming to a landing or meeting with anyone, and the interminable steps began to grow monotonous. Presently they heard a scuffling and a stamping and a roaring behind them and something or somebody began to push them most rudely until at last the wall gave way, the stairs gave way, they gave way, and tumbled right on to the tips of their noses.

"Out of the way! Out of the way!" screamed a chorus of curious voices, and Maude and Willie found themselves taken by the hand by a weird-looking dwarf with a swivel eye and an elevated proboscis, and led out of danger.

The children could not help gazing upon their preserver, who was so grotesquely formed, with a humped back, twisted legs, very long arms, and such a funny little body without any neck. But his eyes atoned for everything—they sparkled and glinted in their sockets like bright brown diamonds—only there are no brown diamonds, you know, only white and pink ones.

The Dwarf did not appear to mind the wondering looks of the children at all, but patted them on the cheeks and told them not to be frightened. But whether he meant frightened of himself, or of the Birds, Beasts, and Fishes and the Bletherwitch   19

that were hurrying by in such confusing masses, they could not tell. One thing, however, that

astonished them very much was the deference with which they greeted their quaint rescuer, as they passed by. For every creature from the Lion to the Mouse bowed most politely as they approached him, and then went on their way gaily frisking, for this was their weekly half-holiday.

"How do you like my Menagerie," enquired the Dwarf. "Rough and ready, perhaps, but as docile as a flat-iron if you treat them properly."

"It is just like the Zoo," declared Willie. "Or the animals in Æsop's Fables," suggested Maude.

This delighted the Dwarf very much, for though he looked so serious, he was full of good humour and skipped about with much agility.

"Good! Good!" he cried. "Æsop and the Zoo! Ha! Ha! He! He! Anybody can be a Zoo but only one can be Æsop, and I am he!"

"Æsop! Are you really Mr Æsop, the Phrygian Philosopher?" cried Maude.

"*King* Æsop, I should say," corrected Willie. "I am glad we have met you, because now, perhaps, you will kindly tell us what a Fable really is."

"A Fable," said the merry Æsop, with a twinkle in his witty eyes, "is a fictitious story about nothing that ever happened, related by nobody that ever lived. And the moral is, that every one is quite innocent, only they must not do it again!"

"Ah! that is only your fun," said Willie sagely, "because of the moral. Why do they give you so many morals?"

"I don't know," answered Æsop gravely. "But the Commentators and Editors do give a lot of applications and morals to the tales of my animals, don't they?"

"I like a tale with a moral," averred Maude, "it finishes everything up so satisfactorily, I think. Now, Mr Æsop, as you know so much, please tell us what a proverb is?"

"Ah!" replied Mr Æsop, "I don't make proverbs. There are too many already, but a proverb usually seems to me to be something you always theoretically remember to practically forget."

Neither of the children quite understood this, though Maude thought it was what her papa would call satire, and satire was such a strange word that she could never fully comprehend the meaning.

Willie was silent too, like his sister, and seeing them deep in thought, King Æsop waved a little wand he had in his hand, and all the Birds and Beasts and Fishes joined hands and paws, and fins and wings, and danced in a circle singing to the music of a quantity of piping birds in the trees :—

> If you want to be merry and wise,
> You must all be as bright as you can,
>   You never must quarrel,
>   Or spoil a right moral,
> But live on a regular plan.
> You must read, write and arith-metise,
> Or you'll never grow up to be good ;
>   And you mustn't say " Won't,"
>   Or " I shan't " and " I don't,"
> Or disturb the Indicative Mood.
>
>   So round about the Knowledge Tree,
>   Each boy and girl must go,

To learn in school the golden rule,
And Duty's line to toe!

If you want to be clever and smart,
You must also be ready for play,
And don't be too subtle
When batting your shuttle,
But sport in a frolicsome way.
With bat and with ball take your part,
Or with little doll perched on your knee,
You sing all the time,
To a nursery rhyme,
Before you go in to your tea!

So round about the Sunset Tree
Each boy and girl should go
To play a game of—What's its name?
That is each game—you know!

After merrily joining in this very original song, with dancing accompaniment, Maude and Willie thanked King Æsop for permitting his animals to entertain them.

"Always glad to please good little boys and

girls, you know," he replied pleasantly, "even in their play they furnish us with a new fable and a moral."

"And that is?"

"All play and no work makes the world stand still."

Before they could ask for an explanation, their attention was once more drawn to the animals,

who had commenced playing all kinds of games just the same as they themselves played in the play-ground at school. The Toads were playing Leap-frog; the Elephants and the Bears, Fly the Garter; the Dromedaries, Hi! Spie! Hi! while the snakes were trundling their hoops. The Lions and the Lambs were playing at cricket with the Donkeys as fielders and the Wombat as umpire.

The Frogs were in a corner by themselves playing "Kiss in the Ring," and crying out:—
"It isn't you! It isn't you!
We none of us know what to do,"
in a very serio-comic manner. Then the Storks and the Cranes and the Geese and the Ganders were standing in a circle singing:—

>Sally, Sally Waters,
> Sitting in the Moon,
>With the camel's daughters,
> All through the afternoon!
>Oh Sally! Bo Sally!
> Where's your dusting pan;
>My Sally! Fie Sally!
> Here is your young man!

In another part the Crabs, the Sheep, and the Fox, were vowing that London Bridge was Broken Down, because they had not half-a-crown, which seemed a curious reason. Then all the rest of the wild creatures, Birds, Beasts, and Fishes, commenced an extraordinary dance, singing, croaking, flapping their fins and spreading their wings, to these words:—

We are a crowd of jolly boys,
    All romping on the lea;
We always make this merry noise,
    When we return from sea.

So we go round and round and round,
    Because we've come ashore;
For Topsy Turvey we are bound,
    So round again once more.

Go in and out of the coppice,
    Go in and out at the door;
And do not wake the poppies,
    Who want to have a snore.

It was too ridiculous; they could recognise every animal they had read about in Æsop, and they were all behaving in a manner they little dreamed could be possible, out of a Night-mare. But it certainly was not a Night-mare, though they could distinguish several horses and ponies.

They never seemed to stop in their games, and even the Ants and the Gnats were playing—and above all a game of football,—though as some

played according to Association and some to Rugby rules, of course it was rather perplexing to the on-lookers. When they grew tired of watching the Animal World enjoying their holiday, they turned to consult King Æsop, but to their astonishment, he was not near them — he had vanished! And when they turned round the other way the Animals had vanished too, and they were quite alone. Indeed everything seemed to disappear, even the light that had been their guide so long, and they began to tremble with fear and apprehension.

Not a sound was to be heard, and darkness gradually fell around them. They held each other by the hand, and determined to go forward, but to their dismay they could not move! They were glued to the earth. They tried to speak, but their tongues stuck to the roofs of their mouths, and they were in great distress. "Where, Oh where was the Zankiwank?" they wondered in their thoughts. And a buzzing in their ears took up the refrain :—

The Zankiwank, the Zankiwank,
  Oh where, Oh where is the Zankiwank?
He brought us here, and much we fear
  His conduct's far from Franky-wank!
The Zankiwank, the Zankiwank,
  He has gone to seek the Bletherwitch,
Oh the Zankiwank, 'tis a panky prank
  To leave us here to die in a ditch.

"A telegram, did you say? For me, of course, what an age you have been. How is my blushing bride? Let me see—

'*From the Bletherwitch, Nonsuch Street,*
                        To the Zankiwank, Nodland.
Forgot my new shoes, and the housemaid's killed the parrot. Put the kettle on.'"

Then the children heard some sobbing sound soughing through the silence and they knew that they were saved. Also that the Zankiwank was weeping. So with a strong effort Maude managed to call out consolingly, "Zankiwanky, dear! don't cry, come and let me comfort you."

But the Zankiwank refused to be comforted. However, he came forward muttering an incantation of some sort, and Maude and Willie finding themselves free, rushed forward and greeted him.

"Hush, my dears, the Nargalnannacus is afloat on the wild, wild main. We must be careful and depart, or he will turn us into something unpleasant—the last century or may be the next, as it is close at hand, and inexpensive. Follow me to the ship that is waiting in the Bay Window, and we will go and get some Floranges."

Carefully Maudie and Willie followed the Zankiwank, each holding on by the tails of his coat, glad enough to go anywhere out of the Blackness of the Dark.

Soon they found themselves in Window Bay, and climbing up the sides of a mighty ship with five funnels and a red-haired captain.

"Quick," called the Captain, "the Nargalnannacus is on the lee scuppers just off the jibboom brace. Make all sail for the Straights of Ballambangjan, and mind the garden gate."

Then the Zankiwank became the man at the wheel, and the vessel scudded before the wind as the two children went off into a trance.

Part II

The Fairies' Feather and
Flower Land

*Faëry elves,
Whose midnight revels, by a forest side
Or fountain, some belated peasant sees,
Or dreams he sees, while overhead the moon
Sits arbitress.*
MILTON.

*O then I see Queen Mab hath been with you:
She is the fairies' midwife; and she comes
In shape no bigger than an agate-stone
On the fore-finger of an alderman,
Drawn with a train of little atomies,
Athwart men's noses as they lie asleep.*
SHAKESPEARE.

The Fairies' Feather and Flower Land

HOW long Maude and Willie had been rocking in the cradle of the deep they could not tell, nor how long it took them to steam through the Straits of Ballambangjan, for everything was exceptionally bleak and blank to them. By the way, if you cannot find the Straits of Ballambangjan in your Geography or on the Map, you should consult the first sailor you meet, and he will give you as much information on the subject as any boy or girl need require.

Both children experienced that curious sensation of feeling asleep while they were wide awake, and feeling wide awake when they imagined themselves to be asleep, just as one does feel sometimes in the early morning, when the sun is beginning to peep through the blinds, and the starlings are chattering, and the sparrows are tweeting under the eaves, outside the window.

They were no longer on the vessel that had borne them away from Fableland, and the approach of the Nargalnannacus, a fearsome creature whom nobody has yet seen, although most of us may not have heard about him.

The obliging Zankiwank was with them, and when they looked round they found themselves in a square field festooned with the misty curtains of the Elfin Dawn.

"Of course," said the Zankiwank, "this is Midsummer Day, and very soon it will be Midsummer Night, and you will see some wonders that will outwonder all the wonders that wonderful people have ever wondered both before and afterwards. Listen to the Flower-Fairies—not the garden flowers, but the wild-flowers; they will sing you a song, while I beat time—not that there is any real need to beat Time, because he is a most re-

spectable person, though he always contrives to beat us."

Both children would have liked to argue out this speech of the Zankiwank because it puzzled them, and they felt it would not parse properly. However, as just at that moment the Elfin Orchestra appeared, they sat on the grass and listened :—

The Elfin Dawn.

This is the Elfin Dawn,
When ev'ry Fay and Faun,
   Trips o'er the earth with joy and mirth,
And Pleasure takes the maun.
Night's noon stars coyly peep,
O'er dale and dene and deep,
   And Fairies fair float through the air,
Love's festival to keep.

    We dance and sing in the Welkin Ring,
    While Heather Bells go Ding-dong-ding!
      To greet the Elfin Dawn.

> The Flower-fairies spread each wing,
> And trip about with mincing ging,
> Upon the magic lawn.

And so we frisk and play,
Like mortals, in the day ;
From acorn cup we all wake up
Titania to obey.
We never, never die,
And this the reason why,
Of Fancy's art we are the part
That lives eternalie.

> We dance and sing in the Welkin Ring,
> While Heather Bells go Ding-dong-ding!
> To greet the Elfin Dawn.
> The Flower-fairies spread each wing,
> And trip about with mincing ging,
> Upon the magic lawn.

"They keep very good time, don't they?" said the Zankiwank to the children, who were completely entranced with pleasure and surprise.

"Lovely, lovely," was all they could say.

and the Bletherwitch 41

Every wild flower they could think of, and every bird of the air, was to be seen in this

beautiful place with the purling stream running down the centre, crossed by innumerable rustic bridges, while far away they could see a fountain ever sending upward its cooling sprays of crystal water.

"I think I shall spend my honeymoon here," said the Zankiwank. "I have already bought a honeycomb for my bride. I am so impatient to have her by my side that I have dispatched the Jackarandajam and Mr Swinglebinks in a four-wheeled cab to fetch her. When the Bletherwitch arrives I will introduce you, and you shall both be bridesmaids!"

"But I can't be a bridesmaid, you know," corrected Willie.

"Oh yes, you can. You can be anything here you like. You only have to eat some Fern seeds and you become invisible, and nobody would know you. It is so simple, and saves a lot of argument. And you should never argue about anything unless you know nothing about it, then you are sure to win."

"But," interrupted Maude, "how can you know nothing about anything?"

"'Tis the easiest thing out of the world," said the Zankiwank. "What is nothing?"

"Nothing."

"Precisely. Nothing is nothing; but what is better than nothing?"

"Something."

"Wrong! Wrong! Wrong! Where is your logic? Nothing is better than something! I'll prove it:—

> "Nothing is sweeter than honey,
> Nothing's more bitter than gall,
> Nothing that's comic is funny,
> Nothing is shorter than tall."

"That is nonsense and nothing to do with the case," exclaimed Maude.

"Nonsense? Nonsense? Did you say nonsense?"

"Of course she did," said Willie, "and so do I."

"Nonsense! To me? Do you forget what my name is?"

"Oh, no, nothing easier than to remember it. You are the Great Zankiwank."

"Thank you, I am satisfied. I thought you had forgotten. I am not cross with you."

Maude and Willie vowed they would not cross him for anything, let alone nothing, and so the Zankiwank was appeased and offered to give them the correct answer to his own unanswerable conundrum. Do you know what a conundrum is though? I will tell you while the Zankiwank is curling his whiskers :—

A conundrum is an impossible question with an improbable answer. Think it over the next time you read "Robinson Crusoe."

"Nothing is better than a good little girl ;
But a jam tart is better than nothing,
Therefore a jam tart is better than the best little
    girl alive."

"What do you think of that?" said the Zankiwank.

"I have heard something like it before. But that is nothing. Anyhow I would much rather be a little girl than a jam tart—because a jam tart must be sour because it's tart, and a little girl is always sweet," promptly replied Willie, kissing his sister Maude on the nose—but that was an accident, because she moved at the wrong moment.

"You distress me," said the Zankiwank. "Suppose I were to try to shoot Folly as it flies, and hit a Fool's Cap and Bells instead, what would you say?"

"I should say that you had shot at nothing and missed it."

At this Maude and Willie laughed girlsterously and boysterously, and the Zankiwank wept three silent tears in the teeth of the wind and declared that nothing took his fancy so  much as having nothing to take. So they took him by the arm and begged him, as he was so clever and had mentioned the name, to take them to Fancy's dwelling-place.

"I think Fancy must dwell amongst the wild flowers—the sweet beautiful wild flowers that

grow in such charming variety of disorder."
Saying this, Maude took Willie's hand and
urged the Zankiwank forward.

Before the Zankiwank could reply, a company
of fairies, all dressed in pink and green, leapt
from the petals of the flowers and danced forward,
singing to the buzz of the bees and the breaking
note of the yellow-ammer with his bright gamboge
breast :—

WHERE IS FANCY BRED.

O would you know where Fancy dwells?
   And where she flaunts her head?
Come to the daisy-spangled dells,
   And seek her in her bed.
For Fancy is a maiden sweet,
   With all a maiden's whims;
As quick as thought—as Magic fleet—
   Like gossamer she skims.

O seek among the birds and bees,
   And search among the buds;
In babbling brook, in silver seas,
   Or in the raging floods.

Gaze upward to the starry vault;
  Or ask the golden sun :
Though ever you will be at fault
  Before your task is done.

O would you know where Fancy dwells?
  It is not in the flow'rs;
It is not in the chime of bells,
  Nor in the waking hours.
It is not in the learnèd brain,
  Nor in the busy mart;
It lives not with the false and vain,
  But in the tender heart.

As mysteriously as they had appeared, the fairies vanished again, and only the rustling of the leaves and the twittering of the birds making melody all around, reminded the children that they were on enchanted ground. Now and then the bull-frogs would set up a croaking chorus in some marshy land far behind, but as no one could distinguish what they said it did not matter.

O to be here for ever,
With the fairy band,
O to wake up never
From this dreamy land!
For the humblest plant is weighted
With some new perfume,
And the scent of the air drops like some prayer
And mingles with the bloom.
O to be here for ever, and never, never wake.

Was that the music of the spheres they wondered? Somehow it seemed as though their own hearts' echo played to the words that fell so soft, like a fair sweet tender melody of fairies long ago.

The Zankiwank had left them again, to send another telegram, perhaps, and Maude and Willie went rambling through the meadow and down by the brook, where they gathered nuts and berries and sat them down to enjoy a rural feast.

Tiny elves and fairies were constantly coming and going, some driving in wee chariots with ants for horses and oak leaves for carriages. And while all the other flowers seemed quite gay and merry in the sunshine, the Poppies were nodding their scarlet heads and gently dozing, what time some wild Holly Hocks beat to and fro murmuring—

>Sleep! Sleep! Sleep!
> While the corn is ready to reap.
>Sleep! Sleep! Sleep!
> And the lightest hours a-creep.
>Sleep! Sleep! Sleep!
> On the edge of the misty deep.

As they lay upon the bank, to their surprise a procession of birds came along, the two foremost being fine handsome thrushes, carrying a large banner of ivy leaves, on which was inscribed, in letters of red clover, the following legend:—

BEAN-FEAST OF BIRDS
FROM LONDON AND
THE SUBURBS.

"Fancy," said Maude, "all the birds of London Town come to Fairy-land for a change of air!"

"And why not?" asked a saucy Cock-sparrow. "We can't be always singing the same song, so we come here for a change of air, and of course when we get a change of air we return with new melodies. If you were to Reed your books properly you would know that the Pipes of our Organs—our vocal Organs—want tuning occasionally."

Then, without any warning, they all struck up a new song, and marvel of marvels, instead of merely singing like ordinary birds, they sang the words as well. But before giving you the lyric that they voiced so melodiously I must tell you the names of some of the birds they saw, and if you live in London or any large town you will perhaps know several of them by sight, as well as by cognomen. First in the throng were the Mistle-Thrushes and the song Thrushes; the Redwing and the Fieldfare, the Blackbird and the Redstart, and the Redbreast with faithful Jenny Wren; the large family of Titmouse and the merry Chiff-chaff, with his pleasant little song of "Chiff-chaff; chiff-chaff; chiv-chave." The humoursome Wagtails and that rare visitant the Waxwing, hopped along together, followed by the Swallows and the Martins, and a whole posse of Finches of various orders, particularly the Chaffinches who were joking with the Linnets.

Then came the noisy Starlings, the Magpies and the Sparrows chattering incessantly and evidently talking scandal. The sly Jackdaws and the Ravens looking as sleek as Sunday Sextons, but evidently plotting mischief, were also present, in close proximity to the Rooks and the Crows, who were well able to take care of their own caws. Afterwards came the Swifts and the Larks up to all sorts of games. A few Woodpeckers joined their feathered friends, and one Cuckoo was there, because Willie heard him, but he kept somewhere in the background as usual. Owls and Bats and Millards with Wigeons and Pigeons brought up the rear with a few Plovers, including the Lapwing. Jack Snipe came tumbling after in a hurry, with a stranger called the Whimbrel and a Puffin out of breath. There were other birds as well, but I don't think you would know them if I mentioned them. Maude and Willie did not, and they were quite authorities on ornithology, and perhaps you are not.

THE SONG OF THE BIRDS.

We are the birds of London Town,
    Come out to take the air,
To change our coats of grey and brown,
    And trim our feathers rare.

For London fogs so very black
  Our tempers disarrange,
And so we skip with piping trip,
  To have our yearly change.

      Pee wit! Tu! whoo!
        How do you do?
      Tweet! tweet! chip! chip!
      Chiff! chaff! chiff chay!
      Weet wee! weet weet! sweet way!
          Cuckoo!

We sing our songs in London Town,
  To make the workers gay;
And seeds and crumbs they throw us down—
  'Tis all we ask as pay.

We make them think of fields all green
  And long-forgotten things;
Of far-off hopes and dreams a-sheen
  And love with golden wings.

Pee wit! Tu! whoo!
How do you do?
Tweet! tweet! chip! chip!
Chiff! chaff! chiff chay!
Weet wee! weet weet! sweet way!
Cuckoo!

After this very entertaining song each bird stood on one leg, spread one wing, and joined partners for one of the prettiest dances you ever saw. It was called the Birds' Quadrille, and was so charmingly executed that even the flowers left their beds and borders to look on—the fairies peeping meanwhile from the buds to join in the general enjoyment. The voices of the flowers were lifted in gentle cadences to the rhythm of the feathered dancers' featly twists and turns.

How happy the children felt in this beautiful place with all Nature vieing to show her sweetest charms. And how rich and rare were the gems of foliage and tree and humble creeping plants. How easy to forget everything—but joy—in this fairy paradise that Fancy so deftly pictured for

them! Could there be anything sad in Flower Land? They could not believe it possible, and yet when a tiny little fairy stepped from a cluster of wild flowers and sang them the song of the Lily and the Rose, diamond tears stole down the cheeks of the little lass and the little lad.

THE ROSE AND THE LILY.

A tender Rose, so pretty and sleek,
   Loved a Lily pure and white;
And paid his court with breathings meek—
   Watching o'er her day and night.
While the Lily bowed her virgin head,
   The Rose his message sent;
The Lily clung to her lover red,
   And gave her shy consent.

The Violets cooed, and the Hare-bells rang,
   And the Jasmine shook with glee;
While the birds high in the branches sang,
   "Forget not true to be."

Dear Flora came the wedding to see,—
　　The Cowslips had decked the bride,
The Red Rose trembled so nervously—
　　His blushes he could not hide.
The Daisies opened their wee white eyes,
　　The Pinks came down in rows ;
" Forget-me-not ! " the Lily cries,
　" My own, my sweet Moss Rose ! "

　　　　The Violets cooed, and the Hare-bells
　　　　　　rang,
　　　　And the Jasmine shook with glee ;
　　　　While the birds high in the branches
　　　　　　sang,
　　　　　" O may you happy be ! "

The Flower-fairies were gathered there,
　　And every plant as well,
To attend the wedding of this pair
　　So sweet that no pen can tell.
But a cruel wind came sweeping by—
　　The Lily drooped and died. . . .
Then the Red Rose gave one tearful sigh,
　　And joined his Lily bride.

> The Violets wept, and the Hare-bells
>   sobbed,
> The Myrtle and Jasmine sighed ;
> The birds were hushed as their hearts
>   all throbbed
> At the death of the Rose's bride.

Before the children had time to grow too sorrowful, there was a fluttering in the air and a rushing among the plants and flowers as the Zankiwank bounded into their presence, cutting so many capers that they were glad they were not to have mutton for dinner, as certainly all the capers would be destroyed.

The Zankiwank was in very high spirits, and gleefully announced that the Court of the Fairies, with the Queen, was coming, as Sally who lived in somebody's alley had just informed him. Then he burst out singing to a tune, which I daresay you all know, the following foolish words:—

> Of all the flowers that are so smart,
>   There's none like Daffydilly!

She'd be the darling of my heart,
   But she has grown so silly!
There is no wild flower in the land
   That's half so tame as Daisy;
To her I'd give my heart and hand,
   But fear I'd drive her crazy!

And then there is the Cabbage Rose,
   Also the China Aster;
But Buttercup with yellow nose
   Would cause jealous disaster.
Forget-me-not, O Violet dear!
   Primrose, you know my passion!
For all the plants afar—anear
   I court in flowery fashion!

"Oh, please be serious!" cried Willie. "*What* is the matter with you, Mr Zankiwank?"

You will perceive that Willie and Maude were quite at home in their new surroundings, and nothing seemed to surprise them one whit, not even the unexpected which they constantly anticipated.

The Zankiwank only asked permission to send one more telegram to the Bletherwitch, and then he condescended to inform them that Queen Titania was about to pay a visit to the Flowers and the Birds, and sure enough, before he had done speaking, Titania arrived all the way from Athens, with a full train of fairies and elves, accompanied by a fairy band playing fairy music. Robin Goodfellow skipped in advance, while Peaseblossom, Cobweb, Moth, and Mustardseed attended on the lovely Queen.

"Indeed, indeed this must be a Midsummer Night's Dream!"

"Indeed and indeed then it is," mocked the impudent Robin Goodfellow. "The fairies are not dead yet; and they never will die while good little girls and boys, and poets with sweet imaginations, live. But quick, let not the Queen see you! Eat of these Fern Seeds and you will become invisible even to the fairies. They are special seeds of my own growing and warranted to last as long as I choose."

So Maude and Willie ate of the Fern Seeds

and became invisible, even to the Zankiwank, who was dreadfully distressed and went about calling them by name. In a spirit of mischief Willie pinched his exceedingly thin legs, making him jump as high as an April rain-bow, and causing him to be called to order by the Court Usher.

"And now," said Titania, waving her wand and calling the Flowers and Birds to her Court, "let the Jackdaw sing his well-known War Song."

"If you please, your majesty, I have left the music at home and forgotten the words," pleaded the Jackdaw.

"Very well, then

sing it without either or you shall not have a new coat until the Spring."

So the Jackdaw stepped forth and sang as below, while the Rook irreverently cleared his throat above for his friend, and cried "Caw! Caw!"

THE JACKDAW'S JEST.

If peaches grew on apple trees,
    And frogs were made of glass;
And bulls and cows were turned to bees,
    And rooks were made of grass;
If boys and girls were made of figs,
    If figs were made of dates,
Upon the sands they'd dance like grigs
    With bald and oval pates.

If mortals had got proper sense
    And were not quite so mad;
Their mood would make them more intense,
    To make each other glad:
If only they would understand
    The things that no one knows,

They'd live like fairies in the land,
And never come to blows.

"That's a very nice War Song—it's so peaceful and soothing," spake the Queen. "And now call the Poets from Freeland. This is the time for them to renew their licences, though I greatly fear that they have been taking so many liberties of late that any licence I can give them will prove superfluous."

"Superfluous! Superfluous! That *is* a good word," muttered the Zankiwank. "I wonder what it means?" Whereupon he went and asked Robin Goodfellow and all the other Fairies, but as nobody knew, it did not matter, and the Poets arriving at that moment he thought of a number and sat on a toadstool.

Maude recognised several of the Poets who came to have their licences renewed—she had heard of "poetic licence" before, but never dreamed that one had to get the unwritten freedom from Fairyland. But so it was. Several of the Poets seemed to be exorbitant in their demands, and wanted to make their poems all licence, but this Titania would not consent to, so they went away singing, all in tune too, a little piece that Robin Goodfellow said was a Rondel :—

>Life is but a mingled song,
>   Sung in divers keys;
>Sweet and tender, brave and strong,
>   As the heart agrees.
>
>Naught but love each maid will please
>   When emotions throng;
>   Life is but a mingled song,
>Sung in divers keys.
>
>Youth and age nor deem it wrong,
>   Sing with joyous ease,
>That your days you may prolong
>   Freed from Care's decrees.
>Life is but a mingled song
>   Sung in divers keys.

So on their way they went rejoicing — saying pretty things to the fairies, the flowers and the birds, for they are their best friends you know, and they love all Nature with a vast and all-embracing, all-enduring love.

One singer as he went along chanted half-sadly :—

To tell of other's joys the poet sings;
  To tell of Love, its sweets and eke its pain;
The tenderest songs his magic fancy strings,
  Of Love, perchance, that he may never gain.
Hearts may not break and passion may be weak,
But O the grief of Love that dare never speak!

A light-hearted bard then took up the cue and carolled these lines :—

There's so much prose in life that now and then,
  A tender song of pity stirs the heart,
A simple lay of love from fevered pen,
  Makes in some soul the unshed tear-drops start.
Sing, poets! sing for aye your sweetest strain,
For life without its poetry were vain!

Then they all sang together a song of May,

although Queen Titania had declared that it was Midsummer. Perhaps her Midsummer lasts all the year round :—

> When Winter's gone to rest,
> And Spring is our dear guest;
> The Merry May, at break of day,
> Comes in gay garlands drest.
> The brightest smiles she brings—
> Of sweetest hopes she sings
> And trips a-pace with dainty grace
> And lightest fairy wings.

> Joy is the song all Nature sighs,
> Love is the light in maidens' eyes,
> May is love alway:
> The budding branch and nodding tree
> Join in the revels and bow with glee
> To greet the Virgin May.

> While songsters choose and mate,
> And woo their brides in state,
> The youth and maid stroll through the glade
> The birds to emulate!

Then comes the Queen of May,
To hold her court and sway,
   While gallant blades salute the maids,
And whisper secrets gay.

Love is the song all Nature sighs,
While peace gleams in each maiden's eyes,
   Youth is for joy alway!
The laughing rose and lily fair
Their fragrance shed upon the air,
   As though 'twere ever May.

As the Poets went on their happy way, the last one to depart turned to where Maude was standing, and though he could not possibly see her, said gently:—

O grant you, little maiden, your thoughts be aye
      sincere,
   Your dreams turn into actions,
Your pleasures know no sear:
   Your life be flowers and sunshine,
Your days be free from tear.

How happy it made her! And what beautiful things these poets always thought of and said!

"Now, Peaseblossom and Mustard Seed, you may sing that little song that I made for you when we were floating up near the Moon, and then we shall soon have to depart as we have so many calls to make this Midsummer Night."

Neither Willie nor Maude could understand how it could be Midsummer Night, because Midsummer Day was such a long way off —quite six weeks, for this was only yet the month of May. But they did not say anything, because Robin Goodfellow was looking at them, and they knew they were invisible, because they could not even feel themselves — which is a curious sensation, when you come to think of it.

Now, this is the song that Peaseblossom and Mustard Seed sang together in unison—the fairies, led by Robin Goodfellow, joining in the chorus :—

WILL YOU WALK INTO THE GARDEN.

Will you walk into the garden?
  Said the Poppy to the Rose,
Your tender heart don't harden,—
  Do not elevate your nose.
For the Gilly-flower has sent us
  All because of your perfume,
And the Box a case has lent us,
  To make a little room.

    So Rosey! Rosey! sweet little posy
      Come to our garden fête,
    And our little Cock-roaches will lend
        you their coaches,
      So that you mayn't be late.

All the Waterblinks are waiting,
  Just beneath the Dogwood's shade ;

While the Teazle's loudly prating
  To the Madder's little maid !
The old Cranberry grows tartish
  All about a Goosefoot Corn,
But the Primrose, dressed quite smartish,
  Will explain it's but a thorn.

    So Rosey! Rosey! sweet little posy
      Come to our garden fête;
    Our naughty young nettles shall be on
          their fettles,
      All stinging things to bate.

Now for tea there's Perrywinkles
  And some Butterwort and Sedge,
House-leeks and Bird's-nest-binkles,
  With some Sundew from the hedge,
There is Sorrel, Balsam, Mallow,
  Some Milk Wort and Mare's Tail too,
With some Borage and some Sallow,
  Figworts and Violets blue.

    So Rosey! Rosey! sweet little posy,
      Come to our garden fête,

And the Iris and Crocus shall sing us
and joke us
Some humorous things sedate.

"That's all very well," exclaimed the Zankiwank. "Roses are always delightful, especially the Cabbage Roses, because you can eat them for breakfast, but every rose has its drawback . . . Ho! and it's thorn," he added, dancing with pain, for at that moment several rose bushes he was passing by gave him a good pricking.

"Ah!" said Queen Titania, "that is not the way to look at the beautiful things of life. It is because the thorns have roses that we should be thankful, and not find fault because the roses have thorns."

"That is a sentiment that I can endorse—it is a true bill, and almost as good as one of my own," replied Robin Goodfellow saucily; "and now let us wander through the Florange grove and gather some Moranges and Lemons."

Neither Maude nor Willie had heard of Floranges or Moranges, and wondered what sort of fruit

they could be, when their attention was drawn once more to Queen Titania and her court of fairies, who were all seated beneath the greenwood tree eating puddings and pies that Mustard Seed and Peaseblossom and Cobweb were making for them, chanting, as they cooked the pastry by the fire of their own eloquence, this doggerel :—

> First you take a little orange,
>   And you squeeze out all the pips ;
> Then you add a crimson florange,
>   Which you cut up into chips.
> Then you stir them in a porringe,
>   With your tiny finger tips ;
> And you have the finest morange
>   Ever known to mortal lips.

How Willie and Maude longed to taste a morange! The Zankiwank evidently enjoyed the one he had, for he said it tasted just like mango, ice cream, blackberries and plum tart all mixed up together, so that it must have been nice.

After the feast Titania said she must be going,

as she felt certain that there were some invisible mortals present. She could hear them breathing! At this Robin Goodfellow grew nervous, and the children got frightened lest the Queen should discover and punish them for their temerity.

> "Where Christmas pudding's bliss
> 'Tis folly to eat pies,"

cried Robin Goodfellow to divert attention and the fairies at the same time, but the Queen was not satisfied, and ordered a special dress train to carry them away again.

At this moment the two children tumbled off nothing into a vacant space, making the Zankiwank scream out—" It must be the Bletherwitch in the clutches of the Nargalnannacus." But it wasn't, and if it had not been for Robin Goodfellow's presence of mind, I am sure I do not know what would have happened. That lively rascal, however, guessing that he had used the wrong seeds, at once stepped forward, and taking Maude and Willie each by the hand, boldly presented them to Her Majesty as being favoured mortals

who were friends of the Zankiwank, and so the Queen received them and asked them more questions than you could find in any school book. None of which they answered, because when they turned round the Queen and all her court had vanished, and only the Zankiwank was to be seen.

The Zankiwank took no notice of them whatever, and behaved just as though he could not see them. They called him by name without arousing his attention, for he was once more writing a telegram, only he did not know where to send it. In the distance Maude could hear the sound of voices, and she declared she could recognise the Queen singing, though Willie said it must have been her imagination because he could not. However, this is what Maude said she heard :—

> Dear little maid, may joy be thine
> As through your life you go ;
> Let Truth and Peace each act design,
> That Hope turn not to woe.

> Dream if you will in maiden prime,
>   But let each dream be true;
> For idle hopes waste golden time,
>   That won't return to you.
>
> In after years when ways divide,
>   And Love dispels each tear,
> Know in some breast there will abide
>   A thought for you sincere.
>
> So strive, dear maid, to play your part,
>   With noble aim and deed;
> Let sweetness ever sway your heart,
>   And so I give you speed.

While Maudie was pondering over the meaning of these words, she was suddenly lifted off her feet, and, when she recovered from the shock, found herself with Willie in a balloon, while down below the Zankiwank was fondly embracing the Jackarandajam, who had just arrived with a whole army of odd-looking people, including Jack-the-Giant-Killer, Tom Thumb, Blue Beard, and all his wives, with Sister Anne, Dick Whitting-

ton, and his black cat, and Tom Tiddler, and about three thousand four hundred and five goblins and sprites, who all commenced running a race up and down the valley from which they were fast speeding.

"Keep the pot a-boiling; keep the pot a-boiling," bawled the Zankiwank, and away they all went again, helter skelter, in and out, and up and down, like skaters on a rink.

Gradually the balloon altered its course, and instead of going up it went straight ahead to a large inpenetrable wall that seemed to threaten them with destruction; while, to the annoyance of both Maude and Willie, they could hear the revellers down below dancing and singing as though they were in no jeopardy. And if the words had been correct they would have declared that it was the Mariners of England who were singing their own song:—

> You sleepy little mortals,
>   High up in a balloon,
> You soon will pass the portals,
>   Beyond the crescent moon.

Then Shadowland will come in view,
  A dream within a dream ;
    So keep in your sleep
      While we keep up the steam ;
      While the midnight hours are all a-creep,
    And we are all a-beam.

The spirits of the fairies
  This eve are very bright,
For in your nest the mare is
  Who only rides by night.
Into a magic sphere you go,
  A dream within a dream.
    So keep in your sleep,
      While we keep up the steam,
      For Shadow Land is deep and steep,
    And we are all a-beam.

With a bump, and a thump, and a jump, the balloon burst against the wall, and Maude and Willie felt themselves dropping, dropping, dropping, until the Zankiwank bounced up and caught them both in his arms, saying as he rushed forward :—

"Quick, the gates are only open for five seconds once a week, and if we don't get inside at once we shall be jammed in the door-way."

So into Shadow Land they tumbled as the porter mumbled and grumbled and shut the gate with a boom and a bang after them.

Part III

A Visit to Shadow Land

Swift as a shadow, short as any dream;
Bright as the lightning in the collied night,
That, in a spleen, unfolds both heaven and earth,
And ere a man hath power to say " Behold!"
The jaws of darkness do devour it up:
So quick bright things come to confusion.

       SHAKESPEARE.

There's a crushing and a crashing—there's a flaring
  and a flashing,
There's a rushing and a dashing, as if crowds were
  hurrying by—
There's a screaming and a shouting, as a multitude
  was routing,
And phantom forms were flouting the blackness of
  the sky,
And in mockery their voices are lifted wild and
  high,
 As they lilt a merry measure while they fly.

       J. L. FORREST.

A Visit to Shadow Land

"THIS," cheerily explained the Zankiwank, "is Shadow Land, where everything is mist, though nothing is ever found, because nothing is ever lost, for you cannot lose nothing unless you have nothing to gain. Consequently I shall leave you to find out everything else," with which nonsensical introduction the Zankiwank caught hold of the wings of a house, sprang on to the gables, and flew down the nearest chimney, followed by all the dancers they had seen below, including the Jackarandajam and all the residents from Story-Book Land of whom you can think. But if you cannot think of all of them yourself, ask your sisters to think for you.

It certainly was a Land of Shadows, where revolving lights like flashes from a lighthouse sent all sorts of varying rays right through the mists, presenting to them a fresh panorama of views every other minute or so. The shadows danced all through the place, which seemed like a large plateau or table-land, near a magnificent stretch of ocean which they could see before them with ships passing to and fro incessantly. And all the time, goblins, hob, nob and otherwise, red, blue, and green, kept rushing backwards and forwards, sometimes with a whole school of children following madly in their wake. Such a dashing and a crashing was never seen or heard before, and as each creature carried his shadow with him, you can just imagine what a lot of lights and shades there must have been. Occasionally there would be a slight lull in the excitement, and the racing and the rushing would cease for awhile. Each time that there was a pause in the seemingly endless races, a quaint round-faced little person, dressed in short petticoats, sky blue stockings and a crimson peaked hat, stepped from Nowhere in particular, and either sang a song herself or

introduced a small girl spirit, or boy spirit, who did so for her.

The first time, she descended on to the plateau on a broom, and introduced herself by throwing a light from the magic lantern which she carried, on to a sheet of water which she unfolded, and thereon appeared this announcement:—

I AM THE GREAT LITTLE WINNY WEG.

But as neither Willie nor Maude knew what a Winny Weg was, they were necessarily compelled to await further developments. However, as none came, they listened carefully to her song, which, as far as I can remember, was like this:—

THE FUNNY LITTLE MAN.

I am going to tell a story of a little girl I knew,
She had a little sweetheart no bigger than my shoe;
She used to sit and sew all day—he used to run and play,
And when she tried to chide him, this is all that he would say:

O my! Here's such a jolly spree!
Sally Water's coming with Jack Sheppard into tea,
She's bringing Baby Bunting with old Mother Hubbard's Dog,
And little Jacky Horner with the Roly Poly Frog.
O my! it fills my heart with glee!
The House that Jack is building isn't big enough for me!

In time these two got married and they took a little house,
And soon a tiny baby came, no bigger than a mouse;
But still the little husband played at skipping rope and top
With all the little girls and boys, and drank their ginger-pop.

O my! this funny little Sam
Thought the world was bread and cheese, and all the trees were jam;

He stood his baby on its head, and played at shuttlecock,
And then he rocked himself to sleep with cakes of almond-rock.
O my! he was a sniggadee!
He went to bed at one o'clock and rose at half-past three.

Now once they gave a party, and sweet Cinderella came
With Blue Beard and Red Riding Hood and little What's-His-Name;
And Nelly Bly who winked her eye and Greedy Tommy Stout,
Bo-Peep and Tam O'Shanter, and likewise Colin Clout.

O my! it was a jolly spree!
Ev'ry one from Fairy Land and Fiddle Faddle Fee,
And Mary brought her Little Lamb, from which they all had chops,

While Puck and Cupid served them with some hot
    boiled acid drops.
O my! it was a happy spread,
They all sat down on toadstools and in mushrooms
    went to bed.

As time went on, and he grew grey, he took to
    flying kites,
And then he took to staying out so very late o'
    nights!
One day he thought he was a bird and flew up in
    the air,
And if you listen you will hear singing now up
    there:—

O my! I'm such a funny Coon,
I'm going to get some green cheese away up in
    the Moon;
I'm going to see the Evening Star, to ask him
    why he blinks,
Also the Sun to ascertain about the things she
    thinks.

O my! I feel so gay and free,
I'm going to call on Father Time and then return
    to tea.

The two children were so absorbed in listening to this rhyming rigmarole that they did not observe the Winny Weg depart, though, when they came to think of it, the last verse was sung in the clouds, and presumably by the Funny Little Man himself, and they quite longed for him to pay them a call. But he didn't, so the goblins started off once more on their wild career, this time on horseback, making such a hammering and a clattering as almost to deafen them.

Quickly in the rear of the white horses and the spirits, who all wore little round caps with tassels at the top, came a procession of dolls—wax dolls, wooden dolls, and saw-dust dolls, very finely dressed, with here and there a doll who had lost a leg, or an arm, or a head, while some were quite cripples, and had to be carried by a train of tiny girls in very short frocks and very long sashes. At the head of these appeared the Winny Weg again, and just as they were vanishing in the shadows, a regular shower of broken dolls came down in dreadful disorder, causing the children to break from their ranks to gather up their property, as the dolls, it was evident, were their own old companions which they had discarded when new ones were given to them. One particularly disreputable doll, with a broken nose and a

very battered body, was claimed by the prettiest child of all, and as she picked it up, she stepped into the centre of a ring formed by her school-fellows, and recited to them this pathetic poem:—

THE UNFORTUNATE DOLL.

O poor Dolly! O pitty sing!
    An' did um have a fall?
Some more tourt plaster I must bling
    Or else oo'll squeam and squall!
I never knew a doll like oo—
    Oo must have been made yong;
I don't fink oo were born twite new—
    Oo never have been stwong!

I held oo to the fire one day
    To make oose body warm;
And melted oose poor nose away—
    And then oo lost oose form.
Yen some yude boy, to my surplise,
    Said oo had dot a stwint;
And yen he painted both oose eyes
    And wapped oo up in lint.

Your yosey cheeks were nets to fade,
   Oose blush bedan to do;
And now I'm welly much aflaid
   Oose lost oose big yight toe.
Oose left leg is no longer left,
   Oose yight arm's left oo too;
And of your charm oo is beyeft,
   And no doll tums to woo!

And oose a hollow little fing,
   Oose saw-dust has yun out;
Your stweak is gone, oo cannot sing,
   Oose lips tan't form a pout.
Oose hair is dyed, an' all is done,
   Oose ears are in oose neck;
An' so my Dolly, darling one,
   Oo *is* a fearful weck.
It is too bad—I loved oo so—
   That oo should die so soon,
An' to the told, told drave must do
   This velly afternoon!

After this affecting recital they all took out

their "hankelwiches," as the owner of the Unfortunate Doll said, and placing themselves in line, they followed, as mourners, the remains of the

deceased doll to the end of a back garden, which some of the goblins had brought in with them. Then everything faded away again, and more shadows danced on the land and the sea, until nothing was to be seen but the galloping sprites and the Winny Weg, who was dancing in a corner all by herself.

A pink light now burst through the haze, the goblins rode off, and a perfect fairy-land nursery

was unfolded before Maude and Willie, who were reclining peacefully on a golden couch with silver cushions. They had no desire to talk, but were content to drink in all that they saw rapturously and silently. The nursery was crowded, wee baby-kins were crawling about everywhere, with a dozen coy cupid-like dots with bows and arrows. And right away at the back a beautiful garden was disclosed, in which happy young couples were seen perambulating arm-in-arm, talking soft nothings to each other. Meanwhile

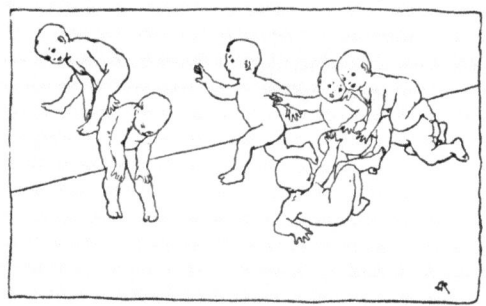

the crawling babies in the Universal Nursery began to stand up; and then commenced such a game of leap-frog by these tiny mites, that made even the Cheshire Cat smile. It was so funny to hear these dots call out to each other to tuck in their "tuppennies," and to see them flying, without stopping to take breath, over each other's backs. Even the little pink and blue cupids laughed until the babies crept back to their cribs once more, and were rocked off to sleep as the Winny Weg waved her wand, and an unseen choir of little girls and boys was heard singing this Lullaby:—

O WE ARE SO SLEEPY!

O we are so sleepy!
   Blinky, winky eyes:
Why are you so peepy
   Ere the twilight dies?
See! the dustman calleth
   As the shadows creep;
Eve's dark mantle falleth,
   And we long to sleep.

    To sleep! To sleep!
   O we are so sleepy!
    Blinky, winky eyes:
   Why are you so peepy
    Ere the twilight dies?

O we are so sleepy:
   Nodding is each head,
Playing at bo-peepy,
   Now the day is sped.
Birdies in their nesties
   Rest in slumber deep;
Nodland's full of guesties
   When we go to sleep.

      To sleep! To sleep!
      O we are so sleepy!
        Blinky, winky eyes:
      Why are you so peepy
        When the twilight dies?

The slight mist that had descended went up just like a gauze curtain, bringing into view again the lovely garden reposing in the rear in a beautiful green bath of light.

Then the merry Winny Weg caught hold of the cupids and incited them to dance a slow gavotte, and as they danced they warbled lusciously:—

CUPID'S GARDEN.

O chaste and sweet are the flowers that blow
    In Cupid's Garden fair;
Shy Pansies for thoughts in clusters grow,
    And Lilies pure and rare.
Violets white, and Violets blue,
    And budding Roses red,
With Orange-bloom of tend'rest hue
    Their fragrance gently spread.

Other voices, which seemed to belong to the lads and lasses in the garden, joined in the chorus:—

    Love is born of the Lily and Rose,
        Love in a garden springs;
    With maidens pure and bright it grows,
        And in all hearts it sings.

Love lies Bleeding with Maiden's Blush,
    Sighing Forget-me-not;
While the Gentle Heart with crimson flush
    Peeps from its cooling grot.

And Love lies dreaming in idleness
    To gain its own Heart's-Ease;
The Zephyrs breathe with shy caress,
    Each youthful breast to please.

    Love is born of the Lily and Rose,
        Love in a garden springs;
    With maidens pure and bright it grows,
        And for all hearts it sings.

How delicious and soothing Shadow Land was! Shadow Land! The Land of Yesterday, To-Day and To-morrow. The Land of Hope, and Joy and Peace. The two children wandered off, as it were, into a dream for a time, and when they gazed again, the garden was more delightful than ever—a joyous blend of Spring and Summer seemed to invade the grounds, while many of the flowers and trees showed slight signs of Autumn tinting. In one corner of the garden a magnificent marble and bronze fountain unexpectedly sprang up through the ground and played unceasingly to the ethereal skies. Merry children danced and played around its base, and lovers young and old promenaded affectionately up and down the innumerable groves, stopping now and then to offer each other a draught of the sparkling water that fell so deliciously into the amber cups.

There were no shadows now. All was bright and glorious; sunlight and pleasure reigned supreme. From the clouds unseen singers sang softly to the people as they passed and repassed, and this was the story of their song :—

> In a garden stood a fountain,
>   Sparkling in the noon-day sun,
> Rising like a crystal mountain—
>   Never ceasing—never done!
> Happy children came there playing,
>   Laughing in their frolic glee ;
> 'Mong the flow'rs and brambles straying,
>   Tasting life's sweet ecstasy.
>
>> O fountain pure and bright,
>>   Dance in the joyous sun ;
>> And sparkle in your might,
>>   Until all life is done.

H

In the summer came the lovers,
　　Plighting troth beneath its shade ;
Warm heart's secret each discovers—
　　Happy youth and happy maid !
Plays the fount so soft and featly
　　In the breeze of waning day,
As the lovers whisper sweetly,
　　" I will love you, love alway."

　　　　O fountain pure and bright,
　　　　　　Dance in the joyous sun ;
　　　　And sparkle in your might
　　　　　　Until all life is done.

In the winter, cold and dreary,
　　Cease the waters in their play ;
But the lovers, grey and weary,
　　Seek the tryst of yesterday !
Time and tide flow on for ever,
　　Heedless of man's joy or pain ;
But beyond the tideless river
　　Trusting hearts will meet again.

> O fountain pure and bright,
> Dance in the joyous sun;
> And sparkle in your might,
> Until all life is done.

The voices faded and died away; the scene changed and a purple curtain descended, hiding everything and everybody except the Winny Weg. An extraordinary commotion outside warned the half-dozing children that a fresh flight of goblins might be expected. And sure enough in stalked an army of giants from one side, who were met by an army of dwarfs from the other, the latter on stilts. But the curious thing about them was that the giants had only got one eye, which was stuck on the ends of their noses, while the dwarfs had their eyes where their ears ought to be, and their ears in the place usually reserved for the eyes. Besides which they each had a large horn fixed in the middle of their foreheads.

Both armies expressed surprise at seeing each other, the leaders of which said quite calmly, as though they were asking one another to have a penny bun cut up in four between them—both said quite calmly—

" I suppose we must fight now we have met?"

Upon hearing this the Winny Weg mounted her broom-stick and flew up out of harm's way.

And then commenced the most terrible battle ever seen on land or sea. They fought with penknives and darning-needles, the battle lasted half an hour, and only one stilt was injured. So they began again, using coal scuttles and tongs, and the din was so fearful, and the giants and the dwarfs got so mixed up that a railway train filled with Shadows of the Past rushed on and sent both armies flying. Then the shadows deepened and deepened, and the lightning flashed, the thunders crashed, the sea roared, and a great red cavern opened and swallowed up everything, including Maude and Willie, who certainly were not quite awake to what was going forward, and all they could recollect of the occurrence was that they saw the winkles and the shrimps on the sea-shore playing at bowls with the cockles.

Part IV

The Land of Topsy Turvey

In the noon of night, o'er the stormy hills
  The fairy minstrels play ;
And the strains replete with fantastic dreams,
  On the wild gusts flit away.
Then the sleeper thinks, as the dreamful song
  On the blast to his slumber comes,
That his nose as the church's spire is long,
  And like its organ hums !

R. D. WILLIAMS.

Wouldst know what tricks, by the pale moonlight,
  Are played by one, the merry little Sprite ?
I wing through air from the camp to the court,
From King to clown, and of all make sport,
  Singing I am the Sprite
  Of the merry midnight
Who laughs at weak mortals and loves the moon-
    light.

THOMAS MOORE.

The Land of Topsy Turvey

IF Maude and Willie had been in a state of somnolency during their sojourn in Shadow Land, they felt themselves very much awake on reaching the land of Topsy Turvey. They knew they were in Topsy Turvey Land because they were greeted with a jingling chorus to that effect immediately they opened their eyes:—

> O this is Topsy Turvey Land,
> Where ev'ry one is gay and bland,
>   And day is always night.
> We welcome to all strangers give,
> For by their custom we must live,
>   Because we're so polite.

O this is Topsy Turvey Land,
And all our goods are in demand,
  By mortal, fay and sprite.
Our novelties are warranted,
And through the land their fame is spread,
  Because we're so polite.

Surely they had been whisked back to Charing Cross again without knowing it? The long wide thoroughfare in which the children now found themselves was just like one of the main shopping streets in London. Some parts reminded them of Regent Street, some of the Strand, and some of Oxford Street. Yes, and there was the Lowther Arcade, only somehow a little different. It was odd. Toy shops, novelty stores, picture shops, and shops of all sorts and sizes greeted them on either hand. Moreover, there were the shopkeepers and their assistants, and crowds of people hurrying by, jostling the loungers and the gazers; and the one policeman, who was talking to a fat person in a print gown who was standing at the area steps of the only private house they could

see. They were wondering what they should do when the policeman cried out :—

"Come along there! Now then, move on!" How rude of him. However, they "moved on," and were nearly knocked down by the Zankiwank, who darted into the post-office to receive a telegram and to send one in reply.

They followed him, of course; they knew the telegram was from the Bletherwitch, and the Zankiwank read it out to them :—

"Fashions in bonnets changed. Have ordered six mops. Don't forget the cauliflower. Postpone the wedding at once. No cards."

"Now what does that mean," murmured the expectant bridegroom. "My Bletherwitch cannot be well. I'll send her some cough lozenges." So he wrote a reply and despatched it :—

"Take some cough drops every five minutes. Have ordered cucumber for supper. Pay the cabman and come by electricity."

"That certainly should induce her to come, don't you think so? She is so very sensitive. Well, I must not be impatient, she is exceedingly

charming when you catch her in the right mood."

Maude scarcely believed that the Bletherwitch could possess so many charms, or she would not keep her future husband waiting so long for her. But she knew it was useless offering any advice on so delicate a subject, so she and Willie begged the Zankiwank to be their guide and to show them the Lions of Topsy Turvey, which he readily agreed to do.

And now, as they left the post-office, they turned their attention to the shops and were surprised to read the names over the windows of several individuals they had already met in the train. For instance, the Wimble lived next door to the Wamble, and each one had printed in the window a very curious legend.

This is what the Wamble had :—

> GOOD RESOLUTIONS BOUGHT, SOLD
> AND EXCHANGED.
>
> A FEW BAD, AND SOME SLIGHTLY DAMAGED,
> TO BE DISPOSED OF—A BARGAIN.
>
> *No connection with the business next door.*

While the Wimble stated the nature of his wares as follows :—

BAD RESOLUTIONS BOUGHT, SOLD
AND EXCHANGED.

A FEW GOOD, AND SOME SLIGHTLY INDIFFERENT,
TO BE DISPOSED OF—A BARGAIN.

No connection with the business next door.

"No connection with the business next door," repeated Willie.

"Why, you told us that they were brothers—twins," indignantly cried Maude.

"So they are! So they are! Don't you see they are twins from a family point of view only. In business, of course, they are desperately opposed to each other. That is why they are so prosperous," explained the Zankiwank.

"Are they prosperous? I never heard of such a thing as buying and selling Resolutions. How can one buy a Good Resolution?" enquired Maude.

"Or exchange Bad Resolutions," said Willie. "It is quite wicked."

"Not at all. Not at all. So many people make Good Resolutions and never carry them out, therefore if there were no place where you could dispose of them they would be wasted."

"But Bad Resolutions? Nobody makes Bad Resolutions—at least they ought not to, and I don't believe it is true!"

"Pardon me," interrupted the Zankiwank. "If you make a Good Resolution and don't carry it out—doesn't it become a Bad Resolution? Answer me that."

This, however, was an aspect of the question that had never occurred to them, and they were unable to reply.

"It seems to me to be nonsense—and worse than nonsense—for one brother to deal in Bad Resolutions and the other in Good Resolutions. Why do not they become a Firm and mix the two together?" responded Maude.

"You horrify me! Mix the Good and the Bad together? That would never do. The Best Resolutions in the world would be contaminated if they were all warehoused under one roof. Besides, the Wimble is himself full of Good Resolutions, so that he can mingle with the Bad without suffering any evil, while the Wamble is differently constituted!"

The children did not understand the Zankiwank's argument a bit—it all seemed so ridiculous. A sudden thought occurred to Willie.

"Who, then, collects the Resolutions?"

"Oh, a person of no Resolution whatever. He commenced life with only one Resolution, and he lost it, or it got mislaid, or he never made use of it, or something equally unfortunate, and so he was christened Want of Resolution, and he does the collecting work very well, considering all things."

No doubt the Zankiwank knew what he was talking about, but as the children did not—what did it signify? Therefore they asked no more questions, but went along the street marvelling at all they saw. The next shop at which they stopped was kept by

JORUMGANDER THE YOUNGER,
DEALER IN MAGIC AND MYSTERY.

"Jorumgander the Younger is not of much use now," said the Zankiwank sorrowfully. He chiefly aims at making a mystery of everything, but so many people not engaged in trade make a mystery of nothing every day, that he is sadly handicapped. And most sensible people hate a mystery of any kind, unless it belongs to themselves, so that he finds customers very shy. Once upon a time he would get hold of a simple story and turn it into such a gigantic mystery that all the world would be mystified. But those happy days are gone, and he thinks of turning his business into a company to sell Original Ideas, when he knows where to find them."

"I don't see what good can come of making a mystery of anything—especially if anything is true," sagaciously remarked Maude.

"But *anything* is not true. Nor is *anything* untrue. There is the difficulty. If anything were true, nothing would be untrue, and then where should we be?"

"Nowhere," said Willie without thinking.

"Exactly. That is just where we are now, and a very nice place it is. There is one thing, however, that Jorumgander the Younger—there he is with the pink eye-brows and green nose. Don't say anything about his personal appearance. What I was going to say he will say instead. It is a habit we have occasionally. He is my grandfather, you know."

"Your grandfather! What! that young man? Why, he is not more than twenty-two and three quarters, I'm sure," replied Maude.

"You are right. He *is* twenty-two and three quarters. You don't quite understand our relationships. The boy, as you have no doubt heard, is father to the man. Very well. I am the man. When he was a boy on my aunt's side he was father to me. That's plain enough. He has grown older since then, though he is little more than a boy in discretion still, therefore he is my grandfather."

"How very absurdly you do talk, Mr Zankiwank," laughed Willie; "but here is your grandfather," and at that moment Jorumgander the Younger left his shop and approached them with a case of pens which he offered for sale.

"Try my Magic Pens. They are the best in the market, because there are no others. There is no demand for them, and few folk will have them for a gift. Therefore I can highly recommend them."

"How can you recommend your pens, when you declare that nobody will buy them?" demanded Willie.

"Because they are a novelty. They are Magic Pens, you know, and of course as nobody possesses any, they must be rare. That is logic, I think."

"Buy one," said the Zankiwank, "he has not had any supper yet."

"In what way are they Magic Pens?" enquired Maude.

"Ah! I thought I should find a customer between Michaelmas and May Day," cried Jorumgander the Younger, quite cheerfully. "The beauty of these pens is that they never tell a story."

"But suppose you want to write a story?"

"That is a different thing. If you have the ability to write a story you won't want a Magic Pen. These pens are only for every-day use. For example: if you want to write to your charwoman to tell her you have got the toothache, and you haven't got the toothache, the Magic Pen refuses to lend itself to telling a—a——"

"Crammer," suggested Willie.

"Crammer. Thank you. I don't know what it means, but crammer is the correct word. The Magic Pen will simplify the truth whether you wish to tell it or not."

"I do not understand," whispered Maude.

"Let me try to explain," said Jorumgander the Younger politely. "The Magic Pen will only write exactly what you think—what is in your mind, what you ought to say, whether you wish to or not."

"A very useful article, I am sure," said the Zankiwank. "I gave six dozen away last Christmas, but nobody used them after a few days, and I can't think why."

"Ah!" sighed Jorumgander the Younger, "and I have had all my stock returned on my hands. The first day I opened my shop I sold more than I can remember. And the next morning all the purchasers came and wanted their money back. They said if they wanted to tell the truth, they knew how to do it, and did not want to be taught by an evil-disposed nib. But I am afraid they were not speaking the truth then, at any rate. Here, let me make you a present of one a-piece, and you can write and tell me all about yourselves when you go home. Meanwhile, as the streets are crowded, and our policeman is not looking, let us sing a quiet song to celebrate the event."

> We sing of the Magic Pen
>   That never tells a story,
> That in the hands of men
>   Would lead them on to glory.

> For what you ought to do,
>   And you should all be saying,
> In fact of all things true
>   This pen will be bewraying.

> So let us sing a roundelay—
>   Pop goes the Weazel;
> Treacle's four pence a pound to-day,
>   Which we think should please all.

What the chorus had to do with the song nobody knew, but they all sang it—everybody in the street, and all the customers in the shops as well, and even the policeman sang the last line.

> You take it in your hand
>   And set yourself a-writing;
> No matter what you've planned,
>   The truth 'twill be inditing.
> And thus you cannot fail,
>   To speak your mind correctly,
> And honestly you'll sail,
>   But never indirectly.

> So let us sing a roundelay—
> Pop goes the Weazel;
> Treacle's four pence a pound to-day,
> Which we think will please all!

Again everybody danced and sang till the policeman told them to "move on," when Jorumgander the Younger put up his shutters and went away.

"A most original man," exclaimed the Zankiwank; "he ought to have been a postman!"

"A postman!—why?"

"Because he was always such a capital boy with his letters. He knew his alphabet long before he could spell, and now he knows every letter you can think of."

"I don't see anything very original in that," said Willie. "There are only twenty-six letters in the English language that he can know!"

"Only twenty-six letters! Dear me, why millions of people are writing fresh letters every day, and he knows them all directly he sees them!

I hope you will go to school some day and learn differently from that! Only twenty-six letters," repeated the Zankiwank in wonderment, "only twenty-six letters." Then he cried suddenly, "How convenient it would be if everybody was his own Dictionary!"

"That is impossible. One cannot be a book."

"Oh yes, nothing simpler. Let everybody choose his own words and give his own meaning to them!"

"What use would that be?" asked Willie.

"None whatever, because if you always had

your own meaning you would not want anybody else to be meaning anything! What a lot of trouble that would save! I'll ask the Jackarandajam to make one for me—why, here he is!"

The children recognised the Jackarandajam immediately and shook hands with him.

"I am so glad to see you all. I have just been suffering from a most severe attack of Inspiration."

"How very inexplicable—I beg your pardon," moaned the Zankiwank. "It is a little difficult, but it is, I believe, a strictly proper word—though I do not pretend to know its meaning."

The Jackarandajam accepted the apology by gracefully bowing, though neither felt quite at ease.

"What is the use of saying things you don't mean?" asked Maude.

"None at all, that is the best of it, because we are always doing something without any reason."

To attempt to argue with the Zankiwank Maude knew was futile, so she merely enquired how the Jackarandajam felt after his attack of Inspiration, and what he took for it.

"Nothing," was the simple rejoinder. "It comes and it goes, and there you are—at least most of the time."

"What is Inspiration?" said Willie.

The Zankiwank and the Jackarandajam both shook their heads in a solemn manner, and looked as wise as the Sphinx. Then the former answered slowly and deliberately—

"Inspiration is the sort of thing that comes when you do not fish for it."

"But," said Willie, who did not quite see the force of the explanation, "you can't fish for a great many things and of course nothing comes. How do you manage then?"

This was a decided poser, beating them at their own game, so the Zankiwank sent another telegram, presumably to the Bletherwitch, and the Jackarandajam made a fresh cigarette, which he carefully refrained from smoking. Then he turned to the two children and said mournfully—

"Have you seen my new invention? Ah! it was the result of my recent attack of Inspiration. Come with me and I will show you." Thereupon he led the way to a large square, with a nice garden in the centre, where all the houses had bills outside to inform the passers by that these

DESIRABLE REVOLVING RESIDENCES
WERE TO BE
LET OR SOLD.

"All my property. I had the houses built myself from my own plans. Come inside the first."

So they followed the Jackarandajam and entered the first house.

"The great advantage of these houses," he declared, "is that you can turn them round to meet the sun at will. They are constructed on a new principle, being fixed on a pivot. You see I turn this handle by the hall door, and Hey Presto! we are looking into the back garden, while the kitchen is round at the front!"

And such was the fact! The house would move any way one wished simply by turning the electric handle.

"It is so convenient, you see, if you don't want to be at home to any visitor. When you see anyone coming up the garden path, you move the crank and away you go, and your visitor, to his well-bred consternation, finds himself gazing in at the kitchen window. And then he naturally departs with many misgivings as to the state of his health. Especially if the cook is taken by surprise. You should never take a cook by surprise. It always spoils her photograph."

"Oh dear! Oh dear!" cried Maude, "why will you say such contradictory things! I don't see the sense of having such a house at all. It would upset things so."

"Besides," chimed in Willie, "you would never have any aspect or prospect."

"Are they both good to eat?" said the Jackarandajam, eagerly.

"Of course not. I meant that your house would first be facing the East, and then South, and then West, and then North, and what would be the use of that?"

"No use whatever. That's why we do it. Oh, but do not laugh. We are not quite devoid of reason, because we are all mad!"

"Are you really mad?"

"Yes," was the gay response, "we don't mind it a bit. We are all as crooked as a teetotaler's corkscrew! I am glad you do not like the Revolving Houses, because I am going to sell them to the Clerk of the Weather and his eight new assistants!"

"I did not know the Clerk of the Weather required any assistance," exclaimed Willie, though personally he did not know the Clerk of the Weather.

"Oh yes, he must have assistants. He does things so badly, and with eight more he will, if he is careful, do them worse."

Here was another one of those contradictions that the children could not understand. I hope you can't, because I don't myself, generally. The Jackarandajam went on reflectively:—

"It is bound to happen. The Clerk of the Weather has only one assistant now, and it takes the two of them to do a Prog—Prog—don't interrupt me—a Prog—Prognostication!—phew, what a beautiful word!— Prognostication ten minutes now. Therefore it stands to reason, as the Sun Dial remarked, that nine could do it in much less time!"

"You will excuse me," halloed the Zankiwank down the next door dining-room chimney, "I beg to differ from you. That is to say on the contrary. For instance :—If it takes two people ten minutes to do a prog—you must fill in the rest yourself— prog— of course, as there are so many more to do the same thing, it must take them forty-five minutes."

"What a brain," exclaimed the Jackarandajam, ecstatically; "he ought to have been born a Calculating Machine. He beats Euclid and that fellow named Smith on all points. I never thought of it in the light of multiplying the addition."

"More nonsense," observed Willie to Maude. "What does it all mean?" They looked out of window and saw the Zankiwank arguing with

the Clerk of the Weather and the Weather Cock on top of the vane of a large building outside. Every minute they expected to see them tumble down, but they did not, so to cheer them up the Jackarandajam stood on his head and sang them this comic song:—

THE CLERK OF THE WEATHER.

The Clerk of the Weather went out to walk
   All down Victoria Street;
Of late his ways had caused much talk,
   And chatter indiscreet.
So he donned a suit of mingled sleet,
   With a dash of falling snow,
A rainy tie, and a streaky skye
   Which barked where'er he'd go.

Then, to the surprise of Willie and Maude, the Jackarandajam began to dance wildly, while the Weather Cock sang as follows:—

   O cock-a-doodle-doo!
   The weather will be fine—

> If it does not sleet or hail or snow,
> And if it does not big guns blow,
> And the sun looks out to shine.

The Jackarandajam stood on his head again and sang the second verse :—

> Wrapt up in his thoughts he went along,
> His manner sad and crossed;
> With a windy strain he hummed a song,
> Of thunderbolts and frost.
> He strode with a Barometrical stride,
> With forecasts on his brow;
> Till he tripped up Short upon a slide,
> Which made him vow a vow.

The Weather Cock at once sang the chorus and the Jackarandajam danced as before.

> O Cock-a-doodle-doo!
> The weather will be fine—
> If there is no fog, or drenching rain,
> And thunder does not boom again,
> And the sun looks out to shine.

Now came the third and last verse:—

His prophesies got all mixed and mulled,
  The Moon began to blink;
And all his faculties were dulled
  When he saw the Dog Star wink!
And up on the steeple tall and black
  The Weather Cock he crew!
He crew and he crowed till he fell in the road,
  O cock-a-doodle-doo!

And sure enough the Weather Cock did tumble into the road, and the Clerk of the Weather and the Zankiwank tumbled helter skelter after him. Immediately they got up again and rushed through the window, and catching hold of the children, they whirled them round and round, singing the final chorus all together:—

O cock-a-doodle-doo!
  The weather will be fine—
If lightning does not flash on high,
Nor gloomy be the azure sky,
  And the sun peeps out to shine.

After which they all disappeared except the Zankiwank, and once again they found themselves in the street.

"They were both wrong," muttered the Zankiwank to himself, "and yet one was right."

"How could they both be wrong then? One was right? Very well. Then only one was wrong," corrected Maude.

"No, they were both wrong—because I was the right one after all. Besides, you can't always prove a negative, can you?"

"How tiresome of you! You only mentioned two and now say three. I do not believe you know what you do mean."

"Not often, sometimes, by accident, you know—only do not tell anybody else."

"You are certainly very extraordinary persons—that is all I can say," said Willie. "You do not do anything quite rationally or naturally."

"Naturally. Why should we? We are the great Middle Classes — neither alive nor dead. Betwixt and between. Half and half, you know, for now we are in the Spirit World only known

to poets and children. But do come along, or the bicycles will start without us, and we have an appointment to keep."

Now, how could one even try to tell such an eccentric creature as the Zankiwank that he was all wrong and talking fables and fibs and tarradiddles? Neither of them attempted to correct these erroneous ideas, but wondering where they were going next, Maude and Willie mounted the bicycles that came as if by magic, and rode off at a terrific rate, though they had never ridden a machine before.

They were almost out of breath when the Zankiwank called out "stop," and away went the bicycles, and they found themselves standing in front of an immense edifice with a sign-board swinging from the gambrel roof, on which was painted in large golden letters—

TIME WAS MEANT FOR SLAVES.

There was no opportunity to ascertain what the sign meant, for all at once there darted out of the shop Mr Swinglebinks with whom they had travelled from Charing Cross.

"Don't waste your time like that! Make haste, let me have five minutes. I am in a hurry."

"Have you got five minutes to spare?" asked the Zankiwank of Maude.

"Oh yes," she replied. "Why?"

"Let me have them at once then. A gentleman left twenty-five minutes behind him yesterday and I want to make up half-an-hour for a regular customer!" screamed Mr Swinglebinks to the bewildered children.

"But—but—O what do you mean? I have got five minutes to spare and I'll devote them to you if you like, but I *can't* give them to you as though they were a piece of toffee," answered Maude with much perplexity, while Willie stood awe-struck, not comprehending Mr Swinglebinks in the least.

"Time is a tough customer, you know. He is here, he is there, he is gone! He is, he was, he will be. Yet you cannot trap Time, for he is like a sunbeam," muttered the Zankiwank as though he never was short of Time.

"There, that five minutes is gone — wasted, passed into the vast vacuum of eternity! With my friend Shakespeare of Stratford-on-Avon I can tell you all about time! 'Time travels in divers paces with divers persons. I'll tell you who Time ambles withal, who Time trots withal, who Time gallops withal, and who he stands still withal!' Oh, I know Father Time and all his tricks. I have counted the Sands of Time. I supply him with his Hour Glass. Don't you apprehend me?"

They certainly did not. Mr Swinglebinks was more mystifying than all the other persons they had encountered put together. So they made no reply.

"I am collecting Time. Time, so my copy books told me, was meant for Slaves. I always felt sorry for the Slaves. They have no Time, you know, because it is meant for them. Lots of things are meant for you, only you won't get them. Britons never will be Slaves, so they'll never want for Time. However, as Time was meant for Slaves, I mean to let them have as much as I can. So every spare minute or two I can get, I of course send them over to them."

"It is ridiculous. You cannot measure time and cut off a bit like that," ventured Willie.

"Oh yes, you can. A client of mine was laid up the other day—in fact he was in bed for a fortnight, so, as he had no use for the time he had on hand before him, he just went to sleep and sent ten days round to me!"

"Oh, Mr Zankiwank, what is this gentleman saying?" said Maude.

"It's all perfectly true," answered the Zankiwank. "You often hear of somebody who has half an hour to spare, don't you?"

"Of course."

"Very good. Sometimes you will hear, too, of somebody who has lost ten minutes."

"I see," said Willie.

"And somebody else will tell you they do not know what to do with their Time?"

"Go on," cried both children, more puzzled than ever.

"Well, instead of letting all the Time be wasted, Mr Swinglebinks has opened his exchange to receive all the spare time he can, and this he distributes amongst those who want an hour or a day or a week. But they have to pay for it——"

" Pay for it?"

"Time is money," called out Mr Swinglebinks.

"There you are. If Time is money you can exchange Time for money and money for Time. Is not that feasible?"

Did anybody ever hear of such queer notions? Maude and Willie were quite tired through trying to think the matter out.

Time was meant for slaves.—Time is money.—Time and Tide wait for no man.—Take Time when Time is.—Take Time by the forelock.—Procrastination is the thief of Time.—Killing Time is no murder.—Saving Time is no crime. As quick as thought Mr Swinglebinks exhibited these statements on his swinging sign, one after the other, and then he came to them once again.

"Are you convinced now? Let me have a quarter of an hour to send to the poor slaves. Time was meant for them, you know, and you are using their property without acknowledgment!"

158   The Zankiwank

The Zankiwank looked on as wise as an owl, but said nothing.

"Dear me, how you are wasting your time sitting there doing nothing!" said Mr Swinglebinks distractedly. "Time is money—Time is money. Give me some of the Time you are losing."

"Let us go, Willie," said Maude. "Do not waste any more Time. We have no Time to lose, let alone time to spare! Shall we kill Time?"

She had barely finished speaking when Mr Swinglebinks and his Time Exchange disappeared, and they were alone with the Zankiwank. But not for long, for almost immediately a troop of school children came bounding home from school, but children with the oddest heads and faces ever seen. They were all carrying miniature bellows in their hands, which they were working up and down with great energy.

"Oh, Mr Zankiwank, what is the matter with

those children in short frocks and knickerbockers? Look at their heads!"

The Zankiwank gazed, but expressed no surprise, and yet the children, if they were children, certainly looked very queer, for the boys had got aged, care-worn faces with moustaches and whiskers, while the little girls, in frocks just reaching to their knees, had women's faces, with their hair done up in plaits and chignons and Grecian knot fashion, with elderly bonnets perched on the top.

"That," said the Zankiwank, "is the force of habit."

"What habit, please? It does not suit them," said Maude.

"You are mistaken. Good habits become second nature."

"And what do bad habits become?" queried Willie.

"Bad habits," answered the Zankiwank severely, "become no one."

"And these must be bad habits," exclaimed Willie, pointing to the children, "for they do not become them."

"I thought their clothes fitted them very well."

"We don't mean their clothes," cried Maude. "We mean their general appearance."

"Ah! you are referring to the unnatural history aspect of the case. You mean their heads, of course. They do *not* fit properly. I have noticed it myself. It comes of expecting too much, and overdoing it; it is all the result of what so many people are fond of doing—putting old heads on young shoulders."

So the mystery was out. The old heads were unmistakably on young shoulders. And how very absurd the children looked! Not a bit like happy girls and boys, as they would have been had they possessed their own heads instead of over-grown and over-developed minds and brains. Old heads never do look well on young shoulders, and it is very foolish of people to think they do. It makes them children of a larger growth before their time, and is just as bad as having young heads on old shoulders. The moral of which is, that you should never be older than you are nor younger than you are not.

"But what are they doing with those bellows?" enquired Willie and Maude together.

"Raising the wind," promptly responded the Zankiwank, "or trying to. When folk grow old before their time you will generally find that it is owing to the bother they had in raising the wind to keep the pot boiling."

"But you don't keep the pot boiling with wind," they protested.

"Oh yes you do, in Topsy-Turvey Land, though personally I believe it to be most unright!"

"Un—what?" exclaimed Maude.

"Unright. When a thing is wrong it must be unright. Just the same as when a thing is right it is unwrong."

While the Zankiwank was giving this very lucid explanation the "Old heads on young shoulders" children went sedately and mournfully away, just as a complete train of newspaper carts dashed up to a large establishment with these words printed outside—

ATNAGAGDLINTIT RALINGINGINARMIK
LUSARUMINASSUMIK.

"Good gracious, what awful looking words! It surely must be Welsh?" The two children put the question to the Zankiwank.

"No, that is not Welsh. That is the way the Esquimaux of Greenland speak. It is the name of their paper, and means something to read, interesting news of all sorts. But in this newspaper they never print any news of any sort. They supply the paper to the Topsy-Turveyites

every morning quite blank, so that you can provide yourself with your own news. Being perfectly blank, the editors succeed in pleasing all their subscribers."

"Well, I do not see any advantage in that."

"There you go again!" cried the Zankiwank. "You always want something with an advantage. What's the use of an advantage, I should like to know? You can only lose it. You cannot give it away. Do try to be original. But listen, Nobody's coming."

They both looked round wondering what the Zankiwank meant by his strange perversities, but could not see anyone.

"We can see Nobody," they said.

"Of course. Here he is!"

Well! Was it a shadow? Something was there without a doubt, and certainly without a body. It was a sort of skeleton, or a ghost, or perhaps a Mahatma! But it was not a Mahatma—it was in fact Nobody, of whom you have of course heard.

"At last, at last!" screamed the delighted Zankiwank, "with your eyes wide open and your faculties unimpaired you see NOBODY! And what a memory Nobody has!"

"How can Nobody have a memory? Besides,

we can see Nobody!" said Maude, more perplexed than she had ever been.

"Exactly, Nobody has a charming memory. Memory, as you know, is the sense you forget with it!"

"Memory," corrected Willie, "is the sense, if it is a sense, or impression you remember with."

"Oh, what dreadful Grammar! Remember with! How can you finish a sentence with a preposition? What do you remember with it?" demanded the Zankiwank reprovingly.

"Anything—everything you want to," replied Willie.

"Another preposition! Ah, if we could only remember as easily as we forget!"

"You are wandering from the subject," suggested Maude. "The subject is Nobody, and you have told us nothing about it."

"H'm," said the Zankiwank. "You have confessed that you can see Nobody, therefore I will request him to sing you a topical song. Now keep your attention earnestly directed towards Nobody and listen.

Knowing from past experience that the Zankiwank would have his own way, Maude and Willie, having no one else to think about, thought of Nobody, and to their amazement they heard these words sung as from a long way off, in a very hollow tone of voice:—

NOBODY'S NOTHING TO NOBODY.

O Nobody's Nothing to Nobody,
   And yet he is something too;
Though No-body's No-Body it yet is so odd he
   Always finds nothing to do!

When Nobody does nothing wrong,
   They say it is the cat;
Though Nobody be long and strong
   And very likely fat.
His name is heard from morn till night,
   He's known in ev'ry place;
He does the deeds that are unright,
   Though no one sees his face.

Nobody broke the Dresden vase,
   Nobody ate the cream;

Nobody smashed that pipe of pa's,—
　　It happened in a dream.
Nobody lost Sophia's doll,
　　Nobody fired Jim's gun;
Nobody nearly choked poor Poll—
　　Nobody saw it done!

Nobody cracks the china cups,
　　Nobody steals the spoons;
Nobody in the kitchen sups,
　　Or talks of honeymoons!
Nobody courts the parlour-maid,
　　She told us so herself!
That Nobody, I'm much afraid,
　　Is quite a tricky elf.

For Nobody is any one,
　　That must be very clear;
Yet Nobody's a constant dun,
　　Though no one saw him here.
As Nobody is ever seen
　　In Anybody's shape,
Nobody must be epicene
　　And very like an ape!

For Nobody's Nothing to Nobody,
  And yet he is something too;
Though No-body's No-Body it yet is so odd he
  Always finds nothing to do!

Just as the song was finished, the Zankiwank cried out in alarm—

"There's Somebody coming."

And Nobody disappeared at once, for the children saw Nobody go!

"And now," said the Zankiwank, "we may expect the Griffin from Temple Bar and the Phœnix from Arabia."

A dark shadow enveloped the square in which they were standing; then there was a weird perfume of damp fireworks and saltpetre, and before any one could say Guy Fawkes, the Phœnix rose from his own funeral pyre of faded frankincense, mildewed myrrh, and similar luxuries, and flapped his wings vigorously, just as the Griffin jumped off his pedestal, which he had brought with him, and piped out—

"Here we are again!"

"Once in a thousand years," responded the Phœnix somewhat hoarsely, for he had nearly swallowed some of his own ashes.

The Griffin, as everybody knows, is shaped like an eagle from its legs to the shoulder and the head, while the rest of his body is like that of a lion. The Phœnix is also very much like an intelligent eagle, with gold and crimson plumage and an exceptionally waggish tail. It has the advantage of fifty orifices in his bill, through which he occasionally sings melodious songs to oblige the company. As he never appears to anyone more than once in five hundred years, sometimes, when he has the toothache for instance, only once in a thousand years—which is why he is called a rara avis — if you ever meet him at any time take particular notice of him. And if you can draw, if it is only the long bow, make a sketch of him. He lives chiefly on poets—which is why so many refer to him. He has been a good friend to the poets of all ages, as your cousin William will explain. If you have not got a cousin William, ask some one who has.

Not having the gift of speech, neither of them spoke, but they could sing, and this is what they intended to say, duet-wise :—

    I am a sacred bird, you know,
        And I am a Griffin bold;
    In Arabia the blest
    We feather our own nest,
        To keep us from the cold.

And we're so very fabulous—
　Oh, that's the Griffin straight!
We rise up from the flames,
To play old classic games,
　Like a Phœnix up-to-date!

Then they spread out their wings and executed the most diverting feather dance ever seen out of a pantomime.

I am a watchful bird, you know,
　And I am a Phœnix smart;
From Shakespeare unto Jones—
The Welsh one—who intones,
　We have played a striking part.
For we're so very mystical,
　Both off-springs of the brain;
The Mongoose is our *pere*,
And the Nightmare is our *mere*,
　And we thrive on Fiction Plain!

They repeated their dance and then knocked at the door of the nearest house and begged pantomimically for money, but as it was washing day they were refused. So they went into the cook shop and had some Irish Stew, which did not agree with them. Consequently they sprang into the hash that was simmering on the fire, and were seen no more. Whereupon the Zankiwank looked gooseberrily out of his eyes and murmured as if nothing out of the way or in the way had happened, or the Phœnix or the Griffin had existed—"The Bletherwitch will send me a telegram to say that she will be ready for the ceremony in half-an-hour."

"But where is the Bletherwitch, and how do you know?" asked Maude, somewhat incredulously.

"She is being arrayed for the marriage celebration. At present she is in Spain gathering Spanish onions."

"But Spanish onions don't come from Spain!"

"You are right. It is pickled walnuts she is gathering from the Boot Tree in the scullery. However, that is of no consequence. Let us be joyful as befits the occasion. Who has got any crackers?"

Before any reply could be given a voice in the air screamed out:—"Beware of the Nargalnannacus!" At which the Zankiwank trembled and the whole place seemed to rock to and fro.

"What *is* the Nargalnannacus?"

"It's a noun!"

"How do you mean?"

"A noun is the name of a person, place or thing, I believe?"

"It was yesterday."

"It is to-day. And that is what the Nargalnannacus is. He, She, or It is a person, place or thing, and it travels about, and that is all I know of it. Nobody has ever seen a Nargalnannacus, and nobody ever will, not a real, proper, authen——"

"Authenticated," assisted Maude.

"Thank you—authenticated one. Directly they do they turn yellow and green, and are seen no more."

"What are we to do then?" anxiously enquired Willie.

"The best that offers. We have been expecting an outbreak for a long time, and here comes the Court Physician, Dr Pampleton, to happily confirm my worst suspicions!"

The children thought it extremely odd that having one's worst suspicions confirmed should make any person happy. But they were accustomed to the Zankiwank's curious modes of speech and lack of logic, so that they wisely held their tongues in silence. The newcomer was of very remarkable appearance. He was tall and slim like the Zankiwank, but instead of having the ordinary shaped head and face, he carried on his shoulders a sheep's head, and in his veins (so they heard afterwards) ran sheep's blood. At one period of his existence he had been well-known for his wool-gathering propensities, and he was now strongly recommended as being able to commit more mistakes and blunders in half-an-hour than a school boy could in a whole school term. He had one great virtue, however, and that was that he would always instantly apologise for any error he might make.

He never travelled without his medicine chest,

which he carried by straps over his shoulders, and was prepared to give anybody a dose of physic without the slightest provocation at double charges.

"There is danger ahead," he whispered to the Zankiwank, "and a lot of visitors are coming to fight to the bitter end."

"Tell me their names," cried the Zankiwank excitedly. Whereupon, Dr Pampleton recited them as follows, the Zankiwank groaning as each cognomen was uttered :—

  "The Wollypog" (*groan*)
  "The Fustilug" (*groan*)
  "What's-His-Name" (*groan*)
  "Thing'um-a-Bob" (*groan*)
     and
  "The Woogabblewabble Bogglewoggle
    and all his Court."

The last was too much for the Zankiwank, for he immediately climbed to the top of the tallest steeple in the town, saying with much discretion :—

"I will see that all is fair. I will be the judge."

Maude had only just got time to eat some of the Fern Seeds she had saved from what Robin Goodfellow had given her, and to give some to Willie, when a rushing as of many waters and a roaring as of the bursting of several gasometers were heard, and a noise of some two or three hundred tramping soldiers smote upon their ears, and they knew that something dreadful was going to happen. As the Bogglewoggle and the Wollypog and all the others came upon the scene, both the children recognised them, from what they had once read in a fairy book, as being the monsters of the Secret Cavern.

It was not going to be a battle, as they could see—it was only to be a quiet fight between the important folk of the Secret Cavern and Topsy Turvey Land. The Jorumgander was there, and so was the Jackarandajam and Mr Swinglebinks, and all the others they had been introduced to. The Bogglewoggle was particularly noisy in calling out for the Zankiwank, but as he was engaged to be married, of course he could not risk his life just for the mere whim of a dragon, who was setting everything alight with his torch-like tail.

And then they all commenced to fight—cutting, slashing and crashing each other with double-edged swords, while the inhabitants applauded and the bands played the "Conquering Hero," although there was not any creature who conquered, that one could distinguish. It was a terrible sight. They never ceased for a minute, but went on cutting each other to pieces until at last they all lay dead upon the ground. No one was left alive to tell the awful news but the Zankiwank and Dr Pampleton. And what was most remarkable about the fight was that it was all done out of pure friendship—but friendship does not seem to be much good when all your friends are scattered about, as these were. Heads and arms and legs everywhere, and there certainly did not appear to be much hope of their ever being able to do any more damage.

The Zankiwank crept cautiously down from his pinnacle and joined Dr Pampleton.

"Our friends are very much cut up," said Dr Pampleton.

"What is to be done?" the Zankiwank enquired.

"Done? Why, with my special elixir I shall bring them all to life again," said the Court Physician promptly.

"Will you? Can you?"

"Of course. You get all the bodies and lay them in a line. I'll gather up the heads and stick 'em on with elastic glue. Then you find the arms and legs and we will soon have them ready for another bout."

So the Zankiwank sent the rest of the populace, that had been looking on, indoors to get their tea, while he set to work and did as that absurd old Doctor instructed him.

Willie and Maude could scarcely keep their eyes open, but they were so interested in the proceedings that they managed to see that the Court Physician with his usual foresight was sticking the heads on the wrong bodies, and the arms and legs he put on just as they were handed to him, left on

the right, and right on the left, and no one individual got his own proper limbs fastened to him.

It was the funniest thing they had ever seen—better than any pantomime, for sure enough they all came to life again, and naturally, seeing another person's arms and legs on their bodies, they imagined themselves to be somebody else entirely. And then ensued the most deafening confusion conceivable, each one accusing the other of having robbed him in his sleep, for they were under the impression that they had been to bed in a strange place—and so they had.

It was the grandest transformation scene ever witnessed. The Zankiwank was in deep distress, but Dr Pampleton was in high glee and laughed immoderately.

"Such a funny mistake to make!" he crowed hysterically to the hopping, hobbling, jumping crowd of monsters and dwarfs, who were glaring at each other in a very savage manner.

"I beg your pardon—my fault—all lie down again, and I will cut you up once more and put you together correctly this time," said the Court Physician pleasantly.

"So!" they all bellowed in chorus, "it is you who have done all this mischief. Come on! We will soon rectify your blunder," and with a swish and a swirl they made one simultaneous movement towards the unfortunate Pampleton, and once again Pandemonium was let loose, when high above the din the voice of the Zankiwank was heard calling upon them to have patience and not to disturb the harmony, as the Bletherwitch had arrived at last. Meanwhile everybody rushed madly down the street after the Court Physician.

But the children could see nothing now. Everything was growing dim and dimmer, and the scene was fading, fading away into a blue light. And the last they heard was the Zankiwank speaking tenderly to the Bletherwitch, whom they were not destined to see after all, and saying :—

"Oh, my sweet Blethery, Blethery Bletherwitch! What a Bletherwitching little thing you are!"

Then there was a rumbling and a tumbling, and something stopped suddenly. A light was flashed before their eyes, and hey presto! there was John opening the carriage door for them to get out, and wonder of wonders, there were their dear mother and father standing in the hall of their own home

waiting to receive them. And presently they were being kissed and caressed and petted because, as Mary their nurse said, they had slept in the carriage all the way home from the visit to their grandmama.

This, however, they stoutly denied. They knew better than that, and told their parents of all their adventures, which, as they declared, if they were not true they ought to be, and so they said good-night and dreamt their dreams, if they were dreams, all over again.

THE END.

TURNBULL & SPEARS, PRINTERS, EDINBURGH.

Lightning Source UK Ltd.
Milton Keynes UK
UKHW010721171121
394120UK00001B/214